Praise for *Handjob*

"Erik Patterson's play *Handjob* does indeed include a handjob. So if you're the kind of person who might be offended by that or by male frontal nudity then this play might, oddly, be perfect for you... I don't want to give too much away here because the mechanics of the play, like a whodunnit, depend on audience surprise. Our playwright masterfully plays on what the audience knows, maybe even what they are thinking, and certainly how charged that male nudity is. So a play that's about a handjob, and a little sex work side hustle, becomes about a lot more. Suddenly we're dealing with questions of race and representation and consent and writer's privilege and normalizing gay stories and gun violence. And rather than feeling like it's all a forced mess, it feels like the conversations we need to be having. Erik Patterson is an LA playwright who delights in shocking audiences by pressing against our taboos or prejudices. In some of his earlier plays this passion felt a little clumsy. A bit like an artist who was saying 'I see the world this way and I'm going to shock you with that and I don't care what you think!' The plays had the vitality of a rebellious teenager proudly proclaiming their own voice. *Handjob* is different. You can feel the writer maturing. He cares what we think and he's going to complicate it. If you know Mr. Patterson's work, that's exciting. If you don't, *Handjob* is a great way to start."

—Anthony Byrnes, *KCRW*

"A stunning world premiere... Gets even more witty and even smarter after a big reveal that I won't be spoiling. Suffice to say that Patterson's use of the brazen (to some) title of his play will foreshadow something more over-the-top and in-your-face than your standard theatre fare. Patterson delivers in more ways than one."

—Gil Kaan, *Broadway World*

"Recommended... TOP TEN... Smart and very funny... Genuinely thought-provoking... Patterson's dialogue displays a glorious abundance of sharp wit, and the play's structure is clever and effective."

—Terry Morgan, *Stage Raw*

"We know how to react to theater that's entertaining or thought-provoking. But what about when it makes us profoundly uncomfortable? Attention-getting as it is, the sex is just one of many times that Erik Patterson's dark comedy pulls the rug from under us, compelling us to reassess what we're witnessing. This, in turn, prompts us to consider what's 'authentic,' 'genuine,' or 'real,' mining the subtle distinctions among those terms. Dial out for a look at the big picture, and you might appreciate the way the play grapples with the very nature of theater and how it could or should reflect life."
—Daryl H. Miller, *Los Angeles Times*

"One of the most brilliant pieces of theatre I have ever seen... Patterson's tight and eloquent script is dedicated to drawing the audience in, making us laugh a bit uncomfortably and putting us on notice that there are issues to be discussed. It's about how liberal we, the audience, may think we are. It's about the discomfort of being faced with our own prejudices, no matter how hip and happening we may be."
—Michael Sheehan, *On Stage Los Angeles*

"Hilarious... *Handjob* is one of those rare plays that manages to surprise and startle as much as entertain—and this is a profoundly good thing... I won't reveal the twists and turns—they're ingeniously done, and unexpected. The audience is lulled into thinking it's seeing one kind of play, only to be turned around and led on a merry chase for the rest of the production's 90 or so minutes. The journey is dazzling... It's laugh-out-loud funny until it isn't, and when it stops being funny, it confronts us with ideas we really should think about seriously... Imaginative and funny and outrageous and startling."
—Dan Berkowitz, *The Los Angeles Post*

"Extraordinary, whiz-bang of a script... There is important stuff here... The extended denouement keeps the audience rapt in pin-drop silence. This show is not to be pigeonholed as a 'Gay Play.' It is so much more than that... Electrifying... Don't miss it."
—Paul Myrvold, *Theatre Notes*

"Intelligent as well as emotional... Well written and extremely relevant, challenging and intellectually stimulating dialogue... Kudos."
—Shari Barrett, *Better Lemons*

"Absolutely brilliant, opening up a discourse about why any artist needs to shy away from controversy as it continuously barrages those gathered with uproariously funny dialogue and awkward situations."
—Travis Holder, *Ticket Holders LA*

"An ingeniously structured and remarkably topical script. Yes, there is a scene in which the titular activity is depicted, but the shock value of that scene is intentionally undermined as our frame of reference shifts. Although I'm tempted to be more specific about what happens, the surprises are integral to this theatrical adventure, as we watch the characters try to navigate through contemporary cultural currents, creating plenty of rich, ironic comedy in the process."
—Don Shirley, *LA Observed*

"I was on the edge of my seat... Patterson's dialogue was clever and pointed... *Handjob* capture[s] the magic of what theater can do."
—Ginger Gordon, *USC Annenberg Media*

"A hard look at the human condition... Some of the best writing you will see on-stage... A 90-minute roller coaster ride... There is a tremendous amount to unpack in Patterson's near flawless script... What makes *Handjob* so shocking and uncomfortable is not the adult content, but the characters. They are so human and flawed it is as if the playwright himself is holding a mirror on stage in which we are all forced to confront our own prejudices, bias, and shortcomings... I can't recall the last play I saw that made me engage so heavily in discussion... Easily one of the best-written shows I have seen... You will find yourself thinking about it for weeks to come."
—Mike Reyes, *Mike Check Theater Blog*

Handjob

Plays by Erik Patterson

Tonseisha

Yellow Flesh / Alabaster Rose

Red Light, Green Light

He Asked For It

Sick

I Wanna Hold Your Hand

One of the Nice Ones

Handjob

Books by Erik Patterson

Pop Prompts: 200 Writing Prompts Inspired by Popular Music

Pop Prompts For Swifties: 99 Writing Prompts

Handjob

by Erik Patterson

Camden High Street Books
2023

Handjob is copyright © 2023 by Erik Patterson

Handjob is published by Camden High Street Books

All rights reserved. Except for brief passages quoted in newspaper, magazine, radio or television reviews, no part of this book may be reproduced in any form or by any means, electronic or mechanical, including photocopying or recording, or by an information storage and retrieval system, without permission in writing from the publisher.

Professionals and amateurs are hereby warned that this material, being fully protected under the Copyright Laws of the United States of America and all other countries of the Berne and Universal Copyright Conventions, is subject to a royalty. All rights, including but not limited to, professional, amateur, recording, motion picture, recitation, lecturing, public reading, radio and television broadcasting, and the rights of translation into foreign languages, are expressly reserved. Particular emphasis is placed on the question of readings and all uses of this book by educational institutions, permission for which must be secured from the publisher: camdenhighstreetbooks@gmail.com.

Performance Licensing and Royalty Payments. Amateur and professional performance rights to this Play are strictly reserved. No amateur or professional production groups or individuals may perform this Play without obtaining advance written permission. Required royalty fees must be paid every time the Play is performed before any audience, whether or not it is presented for profit and whether or not admission is charged. All licensing requests and inquiries concerning amateur and professional performance rights should be addressed to the author at erik@erikpatterson.org.

Print ISBN: 978-1-7379853-6-5
eBook ISBN: 979-8-9878016-3-5

Library of Congress Control Number: 2023902607

First Paperback Edition, March 2023

Copy editing by Sherry Angel
Cover image by Mwangi Gatheca on Unsplash
Back cover image by Clay Banks on Unsplash

Printed in the United States of America
Los Angeles, CA
www.erikpatterson.org

PRODUCTION HISTORY

Handjob had its world premiere at The Echo Theater Company (Chris Fields, Artistic Director) in Los Angeles on September 7, 2019. It was directed by Chris Fields. The scenic design was by Amanda Knehans, the costume design was by Ann Closs-Farley, the lighting design was by Jared A. Sayeg, the sound design was by Jeff Gardner, the intimacy coach was Benjamon Toubia, the casting director was Meg Fister, the production stage manager was Rebecca Schoenberg, and it was produced by Chris Fields and Rachael Zambias, with associate producing by Ariel Labasan. The cast was:

KEITH	Steven Culp
EDDIE	Michael Rishawn
KEVIN	Stephen Guarino
BRADLEY	Ryan Nealy
SUSAN	Tamarra Graham
KATE	Gloria Ines
TREVOR	Stephen Guarino
JEFFREY	Ryan Nealy

Cole Taylor took over the role of Eddie midway through the run.

SETTING

An apartment in Chelsea. The time is now.

CHARACTERS

KEITH, 40s-50s, white, a writer, disheveled. Gay.

EDDIE, 20s, black, handsome, fit. Straight.

KEVIN, 40s-50s, white, a writer, disheveled. Gay. The same actor also plays TREVOR.

BRADLEY, 20s, white, fit, beautiful, confident. Fluid. The same actor also plays JEFFREY.

SUSAN, 30s-40s, black, an artist. Queer.

KATE, 20s, any ethnicity, a butch dyke.

NOTES

Urgency.

Words in brackets [like this] should be thought but not spoken.

A right slash " / " indicates overlapping dialogue.

Trevor and Jeffrey should not be listed in the program.

SCENE ONE

A cluttered studio apartment. The man who lives here isn't technically a hoarder, but he's hoarder-adjacent. Two free-standing bookcases divide the kitchen from the rest of the apartment, creating the illusion of two rooms.

The bed is haphazardly made. The bookcases are overflowing. We're talking books literally everywhere*: on the coffee table, on the end tables, next to the bed.* Every-fucking-where.

In the cramped kitchen area: dirty dishes fill the sink. Stacks of unread New Yorkers, along with stacks of mail and unpaid bills.

Two men stand by the bed: EDDIE wears something casual. KEITH seems over-dressed.

KEITH: Thanks for coming over.
EDDIE: You lucked out.

KEITH: Did I?

EDDIE: Definitely.

KEITH: Isn't that kind of cocky?

EDDIE: How so?

KEITH: Just that you—that you think I'm *lucky* to have you here.

EDDIE: I meant my schedule.

KEITH: Your schedule?

EDDIE: I had a cancellation this morning. So when you texted—

KEITH: Oh.

EDDIE: —I was able to come right over. That was lucky.

KEITH: I thought you were commenting on my looks.

EDDIE: No.

KEITH: Thank God.

EDDIE: Miscommunication.

KEITH: I feel like an asshole now.

EDDIE: You don't need to apologize.

KEITH: I hit on this go-go boy once. I asked him to come home with me. He said: "Sorry, I don't go home with people I meet at work." Then he adds: "But don't feel bad, a *hot* guy hit on me last night and I said no to him too."

EDDIE: Ouch.

KEITH: Hey, if you want to get comfortable...

EDDIE: Have you read all these books?

KEITH: I buy them faster than I read them. I've read the ones there—*those* shelves, I've read all those. The ones over there, I'd say about half those. Then that's my "to read" pile.

EDDIE: You could get a Kindle.

KEITH: I like holding a book, smelling the pages, being able to flip back to a specific line. Using a Kindle's like having sex with a doll when you could have the real thing.

Beat.

Do you ever get overwhelmed thinking about all the great books you'll never read?

EDDIE: No.

KEITH: At least if there's ever an apocalypse, I'll have plenty of books to keep me busy.

EDDIE: Are you nervous?

KEITH: When?

EDDIE: Now.

KEITH: No.

EDDIE: You feel comfortable?

KEITH: Yes.

EDDIE: Then the clock's ticking. Better get your money's worth.

KEITH: Oh, speaking of which...

EDDIE: You can pay me at the end.

KEITH: Okay.

EDDIE: You said you had supplies?

KEITH: Yes.

Keith goes into the kitchen area and returns with a box. Eddie glances inside.

EDDIE: You have good stuff.

KEITH: It's everything you said you needed.

EDDIE: Most people don't pay attention to that part of the email.

KEITH: I follow directions well.

EDDIE: Then let's get to it.

Eddie takes his shirt off. Fuck, he's hot. He reaches into the box. Pulls out: rubber gloves.

EDDIE: Safety first, right?

Eddie puts on the gloves, reaches into the box and retrieves a can of Pledge and a rag. Then he...dusts the bookcase.

Keith watches for a bit.

KEITH: Hey, Eddie. What should I do while you clean? I've never done this.

EDDIE: You can watch me. We can talk.

KEITH: That sounds good.

EDDIE: Be normal.

KEITH: Normal. Got it.

It must be strange going into other people's homes and cleaning.

EDDIE: It's a gig.

KEITH: But I mean—seeing how other people live, seeing what they throw away, seeing how they care for their things—or *don't* care for their things, as the case may be—

EDDIE: Trash is trash, dirt is dirt.

KEITH: You know what I mean, though: there's an intimacy there—

EDDIE: You're romanticizing what I do—what you're implying—it's not like that.

KEITH: But you're looking behind the curtain of people's daily lives.

EDDIE: I might *vacuum* the curtains. But I'm not looking behind them.

KEITH: Have you ever cleaned for someone famous?

EDDIE: Do you really think I'd answer that?

KEITH: Okay, don't answer it with words. Blink once for yes, twice for no.

EDDIE: Sorry, man. I'm not playing this game.

KEITH: You would've said no if the answer was no. Which means you *have* cleaned for famous people. Okay, I know you can't say who, but what if I guess it?

EDDIE: I don't get the fascination with famous people.

KEITH: It's harmless.

EDDIE: I was at Starbucks. The guy in front of me looks familiar, this little white dude with tattoos up and down his arms. While we wait for our drinks, I notice people staring at me. It's making me uncomfortable. Then I realize they're looking at *him*. Listening for his order, trying to subtly get his attention. And I don't mean one or two people. Everyone. The barista says "Justin," he takes his coffee and leaves. And then the place erupts. Men, women, old, young, *everyone*. I don't get it. It's a person getting coffee. How is that interesting? How is that exciting?

KEITH: Timberlake?

EDDIE: Bieber.

KEITH: What kind of coffee did he order?

EDDIE: I don't remember.

KEITH: Was he cute in person?

EDDIE: You're missing the point of my story.

KEITH: I get what you're saying but I disagree. Celebrities are part of our collective unconscious. We stare at them on our screens. It's completely natural to stare in the real world too.

EDDIE: I don't know, man. I think it's creepy.

Beat.

KEITH: Have you ever been to the Russian Baths? On 10th?

EDDIE: No.

KEITH: I went the other day. It's a total scene—

EDDIE: How so?

KEITH: Just...so many gay guys. Like, all the gay guys. Every gay guy in the East Village. I walk in and I'm like: *they're all here*. Well, most of them...

EDDIE: What are you saying?

KEITH: ...*you* weren't there.

EDDIE: I'm not gay.

KEITH: You're a shirtless cleaner.

EDDIE: It's a job.

KEITH: A gay sex job.

EDDIE: That's not what this is.

KEITH: But you're *using* sex—

EDDIE: I don't have sex with my clients, so if that's what you're expecting—

KEITH: I *don't* expect that. But you're using sex *appeal*—

EDDIE: My sexuality has nothing to do with this. If you want to pay to look at me while I clean, I'm happy to oblige. It's not gay, it's not sex, it's *cleaning*.

KEITH: Straight cleaning.

EDDIE: If you need to put a label on it.

KEITH: Sorry I made an assumption. Anyway. So I go there. And it's my first time. I walk in and it feels like every gay guy in New York is there, right?

EDDIE: Where were the women?

KEITH: This was on Thursday. Thursdays and Sundays are men only.

EDDIE: Now *that* sounds gay.

KEITH: You get the picture. Speaking of, could you dust those [framed photos].

Eddie dusts a framed photo. Looks at it.

> *It's a picture of Keith with his arm around another man.*

KEITH: *Anyway,* so I'd never been there before. And when I walk in, I feel this thing—this male—this sex *thing*—in the air. Like I feel it on my skin. Everyone's walking around in these little towels, blatantly checking each other out.

EDDIE: That sounds uncomfortable.

KEITH: No, you don't get it, it was great. Have you ever read Armistead Maupin? Being there felt like I was inside his books. Like, classic homo Heaven, you know? There's this towel attendant—straight, definitely straight, aggressively straight—who's playing Spotify on his phone, and as I walk around, checking out guys, his little speaker blares "Time After Time," and it suddenly makes me nostalgic for this moment before it's even over. I go into the dry sauna and there's about seven or eight guys. The only available seat's on the top bench, so I squeeze in. That's when I notice the guy across from me letting his towel...
gently...
fall...
away...
And he lightly brushes his dick with the back of his hand...

EDDIE: Which you took as some sort of come on?

KEITH: Oh, it was a signal. It was definitely a signal.

EDDIE: How can you be sure?

KEITH: Because three seconds later, the whole room's jerking off. It's like porn, but real life.

EDDIE: Where's this story going?

KEITH: Sorry, the dry sauna's just the set-up. So a little later, I'm in the steam room. And there's steam everywhere, so it's hard to see. And I'm not wearing my glasses because, you know, *steam*. I look at the guy next to me, and he isn't covering himself...and he's got this raging erection. I'm talking: the biggest penis I've ever seen, sticking straight up, rock hard. He isn't trying to hide it, he's *flaunting* it, like "hey, look what I got." He's just holding the tip. Like, his hand's just there, cupping the tip of this massive boner. And his entire demeanor, his entire pose—it's like an invitation. So I reach over...

And I grab it...

EDDIE: ...Okay.

KEITH: And that's when I hear—

> *He squeezes a half-empty water bottle on the coffee table. It makes a CRINKLING NOISE.*

EDDIE: What the fuck?

KEITH: He was holding a water bottle in his lap. I fucking FELT UP his WATER BOTTLE.

EDDIE: Holy shit.

KEITH: It was so embarrassing.

EDDIE: You weren't wearing your glasses.

KEITH: And there was so much steam—

EDDIE: So you couldn't see—

KEITH: His water bottle. I felt up HIS FUCKING WATER BOTTLE.

EDDIE: Jesus.

KEITH: Right? I was mortified.

EDDIE: What did he say?

KEITH: I didn't wait for him to say anything! I practically ran out of the room.

EDDIE: Why did you tell me that story?

KEITH: Because it's funny.

EDDIE: But why did you tell it to *me*?

KEITH: I was making conversation.

EDDIE: I'm trying to work.

KEITH: You said I could talk—

EDDIE: Not about dicks.

KEITH: You didn't specify.

EDDIE: It's too much.

KEITH: Too much "gay stuff."

EDDIE: Come on, Keith. I didn't say that.

KEITH: But it's just—you're standing there with your shirt off, cleaning my apartment, and you're acting like this isn't gay, and you don't want me to talk about dicks. Don't you think that's, I don't know, kinda weird?

EDDIE: Look, I'd be more comfortable talking about...anything...if I knew more about you first.

KEITH: So what do you—this is—I mean—what do you mean?

EDDIE: Something personal.

KEITH: The Russian Bath story was personal.

EDDIE: You really think that?

KEITH: I do.

EDDIE: It's a joke. You said it was a / funny story.

KEITH: It really happened.

EDDIE: But it's not like you told me that story so you could connect with me.

KEITH: I'm just making conversation, dude.

EDDIE: Tell me something deeper, then.

KEITH: How deep?

EDDIE: How about this: how about I start? You want to hear something gay?

KEITH: Yes.

EDDIE: Fine. I have this vivid memory from my childhood. When my uncle came out to the family. I didn't realize what was going on at the time.

KEITH: How old were you?

EDDIE: Eight, maybe. I don't know. Nine.

KEITH: Old enough to understand what a gay person is.

EDDIE: But I'd never encountered any at that point—

KEITH: You knew your uncle.

EDDIE: He called the whole family together. So he could tell us all at the same time. And my family, they aren't the most—empathetic people—

KEITH: I'm sorry.

EDDIE: Don't do that. So—my family isn't big, okay? There's my mom, my dad, one uncle, one aunt, my grandma, and me. That's all.

KEITH: What happened?

EDDIE: Right. So he sits us down and he tells us, he says it. And there's this hush. My mom shifts in her seat, to block me from my uncle—like she's protecting me.

KEITH: Jesus.

EDDIE: And then my dad tells him to get help, he needs to see a doctor, he doesn't have to be this way—you know, things like that.

KEITH: I hate that.

EDDIE: And then my grandma says: "The penis sits on top of the balls."

KEITH: What the fuck?

EDDIE: She kept saying it. "The penis sits on top of the balls."

KEITH: I don't get what that's supposed to mean—

EDDIE: She was saying he didn't have one. She was saying he wasn't a man. If he was gay—if he was going to choose to be—

KEITH: It's not a choice.

EDDIE: I'm saying how she felt. She kept saying it. "The penis sits on top of the balls." My uncle tried to get through to her, but she was relentless. He started sobbing and then he left. That's the last time I saw him.

KEITH: He never reached out?

EDDIE: Maybe he tried. I don't know. I was only a kid. They wouldn't talk about him.

KEITH: That's depressing. But, you know, it's not entirely surprising.

EDDIE: Why not?

KEITH: I've heard black families tend to be tougher.

EDDIE: What do you mean?

KEITH: With the whole coming out thing.

EDDIE: Are you about to say you've got a lot of black friends? Because I can't—

KEITH: No, don't quote me on this, it isn't anecdotal, all I'm saying is: I've read a lot of books, remember, and my impression is, among African-Americans, the masculinity issues—it seems like a lot of weight to carry, that's all. I'm sorry you lost your uncle.

EDDIE: Me too. Anyway, that's how you do it.

KEITH: Do what?

EDDIE: Open up. Connect.

KEITH: I'm not sure if—

EDDIE: It's easy. All you have to do is talk. Tell me who you are.

Lights down.

SCENE TWO

The same apartment, but less cluttered. We're in the same place, but also...not.

Two men stand by the bed:

BRADLEY wears tight workout clothes that show off his muscles. KEVIN looks disheveled, in ill-fitting clothes.

KEVIN: So...how do we...

BRADLEY: How do we *what*?

KEVIN: Begin. I haven't done this before.

BRADLEY: You've never done this before?

KEVIN: No. And I'm just, a little—I mean, you're just here for—I mean, this is just—I want to make sure I understand the parameters, is all. This whole thing. This...*you*.

BRADLEY: What about me?

KEVIN: Do you always turn someone else's words into a question?

BRADLEY: I'm trying to get you to say what you want.

KEVIN: I'm just a little nervous, is all.

BRADLEY: Stop using the word "just."

KEVIN: What?

BRADLEY: It's a verbal crutch. An apology.

KEVIN: I don't see how that—

BRADLEY: Maybe you're nervous, but you're not "just" nervous. Throwing the word "just" in front of an emotion takes the power out of what you're saying. And it's not true. We're always multiple things. You can be nervous *and* upset *and* horny at the same time. One emotion might be stronger, but to say you're "just" one of them? It's not true. Don't say it.

KEVIN: I'm nervous.

BRADLEY: That's better.

KEVIN: Right. Okay. I guess I'm just—

(*hearing the word, correcting himself*)

I guess I'm nervous because: you're a whim that I didn't expect to follow through on.

BRADLEY: That sounds so literary.

KEVIN: I can't tell if that's a compliment or a put-down.

BRADLEY: It was an observation. You obviously read a lot.

KEVIN (*looking around at all the books*): How could you tell?

BRADLEY: Funny. You should get a Kindle. You'd have more space in here.

KEVIN: I fucking hate Kindles. I like being able to make notes in the margins, underline things, dog ear the pages.

BRADLEY: Using a Kindle's like having sex with a doll when you could have the real thing.

KEVIN: What I'm trying to say is—this—you. I mean, I saw your ad and I was like wow. Like: what you do—*this*—I didn't know *this* was a thing I could hire someone for.

BRADLEY: You can hire someone to do anything.

KEVIN: When I emailed you, I didn't think you'd reply because—I guess I figured there'd be too much demand, or something?

Because your photo—like I said before: wow.

BRADLEY: Thank you.

KEVIN: I'm trying to say you're hot.

BRADLEY: Yeah, I got that. *Thank you.*

KEVIN: Hot isn't even the right word. I'm a little flummoxed actually seeing you *here in the flesh.*

BRADLEY: I've never flummoxed anyone before.

KEVIN: So you're saying I'm a new frontier...

BRADLEY: The clock's ticking.

KEVIN: Right. Of course.

BRADLEY: You only booked me for an hour, so—

KEVIN: Do you think we need more time?

BRADLEY: Most people book me for two hours.

KEVIN: I can't afford more than one.

BRADLEY: Then let's do this.

Kevin grabs his wallet.

Don't be crude. You can pay me at the end.

KEVIN: Oh. Sorry. Okay.

BRADLEY: You said you had supplies?

KEVIN: Yes.

Kevin goes into the kitchen. Retrieves a box. He returns and puts it on the bed.

Bradley glances inside.

BRADLEY: You have good stuff.
KEVIN: It's everything you said you needed.
BRADLEY: Most people don't pay attention to that part of the email.
KEVIN: What do you mean *people*?
BRADLEY: I don't understand the question.
KEVIN: *People*. Do you do this for women too?
BRADLEY: I do it for anyone who wants me.
KEVIN: So you...like women?
BRADLEY: I'm a fucking pussy hound.
KEVIN: Really?
BRADLEY: I'm cool with whatever. I like when someone wants me. But I live for pussy, yeah.
KEVIN: Okay, that's...Good to know.
BRADLEY: Do you want me, Kevin?
KEVIN: I do.
BRADLEY: That's all that matters.

Bradley strips off his shirt.

KEVIN: Jesus Christ.

>*Bradley's body is ridiculous. The kind of body the internet was made for. Kevin tries to stare without being obvious. Bradley reaches into the box. Pulls out: rubber gloves. He puts them on.*

KEVIN: Safety first, right?

>*Bradley reaches in and retrieves a bottle of Murphy Oil Spray and a rag.*

BRADLEY: Let's do this.

>*Bradley dusts the bookcase. Kevin watches him for a bit.*

KEVIN: Make sure to get the bottom corners.
BRADLEY: Don't worry, I'm thorough.
KEVIN: I only said that because the woman I usually hire to clean—Margarita—sometimes she skips the bottom corners for some reason. I think she doesn't think I'll notice.
BRADLEY: This dust is thick.

(*noticing*)

Hey—*hey*. Kevin. You can look at me, you can watch me.

It's what you're paying me for.

KEVIN: I'm paying you to clean.

BRADLEY: That's not true. I fucking love to clean. I'd do this shit for free. You're paying for the eye candy, so get some sugar while you can and don't make me tell you to watch me again.

(*playfully poking Kevin's stomach*)

Boop.

(*back to cleaning*)

Now back to Margarita: you said she skips the corners?

KEVIN: Only lately. She's been distracted. It's not a big deal. It's— understandable. It's her husband. He died. It was this terrible— accident? Car accident. He was jaywalking. He got hit by a taxi.

BRADLEY: That's horrible. Did they catch the guy, or was it a hit and run?

KEVIN: The driver stopped. He didn't see Margarita's husband— Christopher, that's his name. Chris was wearing dark clothes, it was raining, it was late at night, he'd had a few drinks. It was just—bad conditions.

BRADLEY: The perfect storm.

KEVIN: And she has kids, too—three kids, I think.

BRADLEY: That's awful.

What's her rate?

KEVIN: Thirty an hour.

BRADLEY: Well, that's your problem. Nothing against Margarita, she's clearly going through a lot—

KEVIN: Her husband *died*.

BRADLEY: And I'm sorry if this sounds cold, but you get what you pay for.

KEVIN: Maybe.

BRADLEY: You really *should* pay her more, with all she's going through.

KEVIN: I know, but—

BRADLEY: Honestly, someone has to call you out on this. Don't you have any compassion for what Margarita's going through?

KEVIN: *There is no Margarita.*

(*a torrent of words*)

I've never hired a maid before. A while back, my niece was staying with me and she offers to do laundry. She grabs the dish towels, then motions to the dish rack and says "should I throw that one in with the rest?" That's when I notice the towel under the dish rack, and I say "SURE," but what I'm thinking is: *I've never seen that towel before*. I must've put it there when I got the dish rack, which was: FIVE YEARS AGO. So what I'm saying is: I AM NOT A CLEAN PERSON. I spent hours cleaning this morning to get it ready for you to clean. The state of my apartment right now? It's horrifying and this is after an already extensive, thorough cleaning session. So imagine what it was like before.

BRADLEY: You made up Margarita?

KEVIN: Yes.

BRADLEY: That's fucked up. I was invested in her.

KEVIN: That's why I told you the truth.

BRADLEY: And that stuff with her husband?

KEVIN: I drove into a jaywalker once—years ago, when I lived in Los Angeles—that's where I got that story from.

BRADLEY: You killed a jaywalker?

KEVIN: It was more like I grazed him. He was a child molester.

BRADLEY: So this was some sort of vendetta?

KEVIN: Oh, no—you think I—NO. I didn't know he was a child molester when I drove into him: that was an accident—but then I googled him later and found out about the molestation stuff, which was disturbing. Anyway, none of that happened to Margarita's husband because Margarita doesn't have a husband because I made her up. Are you mad?

BRADLEY: No. I like it.

KEVIN: You do?

BRADLEY: Yeah. It's hot.

KEVIN: Was it racist to call my fictional maid Margarita? I don't even know why I called her that.

BRADLEY: You shouldn't pretend to hire her anymore because she's a really shitty duster.

Beat.

KEVIN: So what should I—do—while you clean?

BRADLEY: Whatever you want.

KEVIN: But what do other guys do?

BRADLEY: They watch...

KEVIN: I can watch.

BRADLEY: They talk...

KEVIN: I'm very good at talking.

BRADLEY: And they ask for what they want.

KEVIN: Can you be more specific?

BRADLEY: You're the one paying. Use your imagination.

KEVIN: I'll start by *just* watching.

(*hearing himself*)

I mean: I'll start by watching.

> *Bradley finishes the bookcase. He goes to the coffee table. Clears off the books and coasters. Wipes it down. Kevin sits on the bed. Watches Bradley carefully put back the books and coasters. Bradley dusts the DVDs next to the TV.*

BRADLEY: What's *The Wire*?

KEVIN: I bought that a million years ago because it's supposed to be great, but I never watched it.

BRADLEY: You know you don't need DVDs anymore, right?

KEVIN: I'm old-fashioned.

(*noticing Bradley smile*)

You think I'm old.

BRADLEY: Age is a state of mind.

KEVIN: When you're 20, age is a state of mind. Once you hit 40, age is a horrifying reality.

BRADLEY: You don't look old.

KEVIN: I feel old.

BRADLEY: And I'm not 20. I'm 23.

Beat.

What do you do?

KEVIN: I'm a writer.

BRADLEY: Did you write any of these books?

KEVIN: Not that kind of writer. I write anything that has dialogue.

BRADLEY: Books have dialogue.

KEVIN: No, I meant—movies, TV, plays. Things that need actors.

BRADLEY: Got it.

Do you want me to vacuum?

KEVIN: Maybe. If there's time. Do the kitchen first.

> *Bradley goes into the kitchen. Kevin follows. Leans against the counter.*

KEVIN: So—how does someone become a shirtless cleaner?

BRADLEY: I'm good at two things: cleaning and fucking. Any day I can get paid for one of those things is a good day in my book. Wanna dry these?

KEVIN: Sure.

> *Bradley tosses him a dish towel. Kevin moves in closer to Bradley. They work side-by-side. Bradley adjusts his dick, which Kevin notices.*

KEVIN: Does your girlfriend know you do this?

BRADLEY: I don't have a girlfriend.

KEVIN: Oh. Because I was wondering what she thinks of all this—if she knows.

BRADLEY: You think I'm lying to you.

KEVIN: No, I don't—

BRADLEY: And even if I was lying, I don't owe you the truth. This is a transaction.
We're not best friends. We're not boyfriends. We're barely acquaintances.

KEVIN: I didn't say we were any of those things—

BRADLEY: I'm here to clean and you're here to watch. So if I say I don't have a girlfriend, then I don't have a girlfriend.
KEVIN: I'm sorry, I get it, you don't have a girlfriend. It's just when I looked you up on Facebook—
BRADLEY: You looked me up on Facebook?
KEVIN: Yeah.
BRADLEY: How? I never told you my last name.
KEVIN: I googled your phone number.
BRADLEY: You googled my phone number?
KEVIN: It was a safety precaution.
BRADLEY: Are you fucking serious? So you found photos of me and my girlfriend.
KEVIN: But I wasn't sure if they were current or not. Jennifer Loftis—
BRADLEY: Don't say her name.
KEVIN: I'm sorry. But the information's out there—
BRADLEY: What else did you find?
KEVIN: Well, aside from your Facebook page, I found: your Instagram, your Twitter, some comments you left in a gamers Forum, and your Reddit account.
BRADLEY: Holy shit.
KEVIN: I also found your secret "throwaway" Reddit account,
your Amazon reviews,
your Tumblr,
a review of the production of Pinocchio you did in seventh grade,
your mother's maiden name,
your father's mother's maiden name,

the name of the street you grew up on,
your current home address,
your mother's home address,
the names of your three older siblings and their spouses, and all of their addresses,
an angry Yelp review you left after a dry cleaner ruined your favorite blue shirt,
your hair color,
your eye color,
your inseam,
your shoe size,
your waist size,
your neck size,
your ring size,
your cock size,
an essay you wrote for a college class where you argued the mathematical impossibility of ever getting caught up on your Netflix queue,
your Netflix queue,
a fanpage dedicated to your band, Late Notice,
a Flickr account full of photos from Late Notice shows,
an actual "late notice" from one of your credit cards,
your YouTube account,
your Vimeo account,
the hospital you were born in,
medical records from the hernia operation you had when you

were eighteen,
your vaccine history,
an overdue parking ticket,
some photos you were tagged in from your cousin Olivia's wedding in Cape Cod,
a masturbation video your cousin Olivia's husband Sam uploaded to PornHub,
your high school transcripts,
your college transcripts,
your elementary school transcripts,
your permanent record, your impermanent record,
your likes and dislikes,
your faves,
your subscriptions,
your pages,
your posts,
your Wikipedia,
your Tinder,
your Snapchat,
your WhatsApp,
your Grubhub,
your Postmates,
your FitBit,
your Grindr,
your Scruff,
your Jackr,

> your Mistr,
>
> your Uber rating,
>
> your Equifax rating,
>
> your Rotten Tomatoes rating,
>
> and your Pinterest.

BRADLEY: Are you done?

KEVIN: Oh, and I also found a dick pic you sent to Jennifer Loftis, who's either your current girlfriend or your ex-girlfriend, that she forwarded to her friend Sarah Stern, who anonymously posted it on 4chan, where someone from Reddit found it, and then because of the way your dick was sticking up out of the green pants you were wearing, it became a meme, and people started photoshopping your dick into significant moments in history.

BRADLEY: You're joking.

KEVIN: No, like they put your dick in that photo of the Migrant Mother from the great depression, and they put it in the photo of the raising of the flag on Iwo Jima, except—

BRADLEY: —they're raising my dick.	KEVIN: —they're raising your dick.

KEVIN: Exactly. Someone put your dick into a photo of Lyndon Johnson getting sworn in on Air Force One, which is my favorite of all your doctored dick pics because your dick's just chilling in the background and it's hard to tell if it's bored or really interested. That's it.

BRADLEY: *That's it.*

KEVIN: Yeah, that's all I found online.

BRADLEY: That's fucked up.

KEVIN: The photos are actually pretty flattering—

BRADLEY: By the way, I don't have a FitBit.

KEVIN: But you get the gist.

BRADLEY: It's fucked up that you know so much about me—

KEVIN: Just what you put online. Things you *chose* to put online.

BRADLEY: You went *out of your way* to find those things.

KEVIN: It didn't take much.

BRADLEY: It's a violation of trust—

KEVIN: I feel like we're going down a negative path here—

BRADLEY: I came into your home without knowing anything about you and thinking you didn't know anything about me—but that wasn't true. So tell me something about you, a secret. Tell me something real, something good, something dangerous. Make it fucking messy.

KEVIN: I don't have any secrets.

BRADLEY: Yes, you do. We all do.

Beat.

KEVIN: I tell people my dad's dead, but the truth is he lives in New Jersey.

Lights out.

SCENE THREE

The same apartment.

Eddie and Keith are where we last left them: Eddie cleans the coffee table, Keith sits on the edge of the bed, watching.

KEITH: I'm a writer.

EDDIE: Professionally?

KEITH: Yeah, I get paid. Not regularly, but, you know, *enough*. It's feast or famine.

EDDIE: Did you write any of those books on your bookshelves?

KEITH: Not that kind of writer. I write anything that has dialogue.

EDDIE: Books have dialogue.

KEITH: No, I meant—movies, TV, plays.

EDDIE: Anything I'd know?

KEITH: Maybe.

(*uncomfortable*)

I don't really wanna...you know...get into all that.

Beat.

Does your girlfriend know you do this?

EDDIE: I don't have a girlfriend.

KEITH: I find that hard to believe.

EDDIE: Why?

KEITH: I figure you probably always have a girlfriend. Like, you must be in strong demand.

EDDIE: Like I'm the latest iPhone or something.

KEITH: All I'm saying is: I imagine you're popular. It's a compliment.

EDDIE: Then, thanks. But I don't have a girlfriend. And I find the question...disingenuous.

KEITH: How so?

EDDIE: You won't open up—you won't tell me what you've written—

KEITH: Because that's my work.

EDDIE: —yet you expect me to tell you everything about my life.

KEITH: That's not—

EDDIE: Do you have a boyfriend?

KEITH: No.

EDDIE: Who's the guy in those pictures?

KEITH: Not my boyfriend.

EDDIE: See, *that*. You closed a door. If you really want to know me, if you want to connect, it's gotta be a two-way street. That's how these things work.

KEITH: I'm sorry. I guess I'm just awkward.

EDDIE: And stop saying the word "just."

KEITH: What?

EDDIE: It's a verbal crutch. An apology.

KEITH: I don't get what you're trying to [say] —

EDDIE: Maybe you're awkward, but you're not "just" awkward. Throwing the word "just" in front of an emotion takes the power out of what you're saying. We're always multiple things. Right now you might feel awkward *and* thoughtful *and* cautious. To say you're "just" one of them—it isn't accurate, and it's manipulative. It's putting emphasis on the emotion you want to carry the most weight. But it's not true. Don't say it.

KEITH: Whoa. I never thought so much about the word "just" before.

EDDIE: I think about shit like that all the time.

KEITH: It must be exhausting.

EDDIE: Dude. *Dude*. You don't even know.

KEITH: So you have a lot of weird things with words?

EDDIE: Look, I don't keep a mental list of pet peeves. But language is a powerful thing and I'm a big believer in saying what you mean. I try to live my life like that.

KEITH: *Say what you mean and mean what you say.*

EDDIE: You make it sound like something my aunt would embroider on a pillow.

KEITH: Don't mock pillow embroideries. More things should be embroidered on pillows.

EDDIE: Embroider *that*.

KEITH: Embroider what?

EDDIE: What you just said. "More things should be embroidered on pillows" should be embroidered on a pillow.

KEITH: I like it. It's so meta.

EDDIE: I'd put my head on that pillow any night.

> *Beat.*

Do you want me to vacuum?
KEITH: Maybe. If there's time. Could you do the kitchen first?

> *Eddie goes into the kitchen, starts the dishes. Keith stays behind. He doesn't want to seem too eager. After a bit, he joins Eddie. But there isn't much room. Where should he stand? It's awkward. He returns to the living room.*

> [This is dumb. I should be in there. I'm paying. I should get my money's worth.]

> *He moves toward the kitchen, but stops himself. Sits on the bed. Grabs his phone. Checks it. Has an idea. He grabs a journal off the bedside table, jots down a few thoughts. Puts down the book.*

> *He goes back into the kitchen. Admires Eddie's torso. He's about to speak. But he stops himself.*

Eddie looks up, smiles. One of those polite acknowledging-the-silence smiles. He returns his focus to the dishes.

Keith moves in closer. Reaches down and grabs Eddie's crotch. Eddie jumps away.

EDDIE: What the fuck are you doing?

KEITH: What? Nothing!

EDDIE: You grabbed me!

KEITH: I'm sorry, I didn't mean to—

EDDIE: I didn't say you could do that.

KEITH: I thought you gave me a signal.

EDDIE: What fucking signal?

KEITH: You smiled—

EDDIE: Are you fucking kidding me?

KEITH: Sorry—

EDDIE: Fuck!

KEITH: I didn't mean to—

EDDIE: No. NO. Who the fuck does that? Fucking "signal." What kind of bullshit is that? Signal.
Fuck.

KEITH: I won't do it again.

EDDIE: See, *this*—fuck. This is what pisses me off about your fucking Russian Bath story. That you can—that you think you can touch anyone—

KEITH: I didn't mean to upset you—

EDDIE: No, don't—DON'T.

KEITH: And how do the baths have anything to do with—

EDDIE: Anyone can go to that fucking sauna, right?

KEITH: Yes. I mean, no—only men.

EDDIE: But any guy can go there, and you don't know that everyone there was gay.

KEITH: No, but—

EDDIE: There's straight guys too.

KEITH: It didn't feel like there were—

EDDIE: But there could've been.

KEITH: Yes, of course—there could've been straight guys.

EDDIE: So what gives you the right to take the place over?

KEITH: I didn't take it over.

EDDIE: All you gay guys—

KEITH: Don't say "gay" like that—

EDDIE: It's what you are—

KEITH: But you make it sound ugly—

EDDIE: Like you made that sauna ugly.

KEITH: I didn't—

EDDIE: You made it a hostile environment—

KEITH: It isn't hostile—it's sensual, it's loving, it's practically *tribal* for god's sake—

EDDIE: It's offensive—

KEITH: Why?

EDDIE: Because if I went to that place and I had to deal with all you horny little fuckers—

KEITH: You don't have to participate—

EDDIE: When all I want to do is *relax*—

KEITH: Then close your eyes and *relax*. Ignore it—

EDDIE: I can't ignore it if it's in my face. That's confrontational—

KEITH: You're the one being confrontational—

EDDIE: No, the whole situation—it's aggressive, it's *gross*—that's what it is—

KEITH: That's not what it was like—

EDDIE: But if someone like me was there—

KEITH: If you were there, none of that stuff would've happened.

EDDIE: Are you sure about that?

KEITH: It would've had a different energy.

EDDIE: Why do I doubt that? Why do I think all you guys would've jerked off anyway?

KEITH: We would've read the room—

EDDIE: Like you read the room just now.

KEITH: I'm sorry I touched you.

EDDIE: You grabbed me.

KEITH: I know. I'm sorry.

EDDIE: Goddamnit.

> *He wants to leave but he hasn't been paid yet; fuck, fuck, fuck.*

Don't do it again, okay?

KEITH: I won't, I promise, I'll be good.

EDDIE: So should I keep cleaning? Or leave?

KEITH: Stay.

EDDIE: As long as you understand my parameters.

KEITH: I do.

EDDIE: You can watch—

KEITH: That's all I'm gonna do.

EDDIE: You can talk about non-dick stuff.

KEITH: Okay.

EDDIE: But you can't touch.

KEITH: Got it.

EDDIE: Now where the fuck is your vacuum cleaner?

Lights out.

SCENE FOUR

The same apartment. Bradley and Kevin are in the kitchen, where we left them.

BRADLEY: Why would you tell people your dad's dead if he really lives in New Jersey?

KEVIN: "The penis sits on top of the balls."

BRADLEY: Excuse me?

KEVIN: That's the last thing he said to me.

BRADLEY: "The penis sits on top of the balls?"

KEVIN: Yeah.

BRADLEY: I don't even understand the context in which someone would say that.

KEVIN: It's what he said when I finally came out. I called this big family meeting. You have to understand that my family—they aren't the most—empathetic people. They're religious, conservative, close-minded. All the cliches. I was nervous. But I finally get out the words. And there's this hush. My mom shifts in her seat. It's subtle, but I see it: she's blocking me from my nephew Tyler. As if she has to protect him. Then my grandma starts crying, she's saying I need help, I don't have to be this way. And my dad's angry. He says: "The penis sits on top of the balls." He keeps saying it. And after awhile, what I realize is: he's saying I don't have one. He's saying I'm not a man. I try to get through to him, but he won't listen. And that's how it's been ever since. My mom came around. But dad won't engage. So I say he's dead. It's easier. "The penis sits on top of the balls. The penis sits on top of the balls. The penis sits on top of the balls."

BRADLEY: Jesus.

KEVIN: Yeah. I never told anyone that story before.

So are we good here?

BRADLEY: Yeah. We're good.

KEVIN: I opened up enough?

BRADLEY: Yeah.

KEVIN: I'm sorry I googled you.

BRADLEY: I already forgot about it.

KEVIN: Do you mind mopping?

BRADLEY: I'm at your service, man.

Kevin grabs a mop and a bucket and hands them to Bradley. Bradley squirts soap into the bucket, fills it with water at the sink. Kevin suddenly feels awkward. He goes back into the living room. Bradley finishes filling up the bucket.

BRADLEY: Listen, if you want—I was thinking...for forty more bucks, I can take my pants off.

KEVIN: Really?

BRADLEY: Yeah. I don't mind.

KEVIN: Okay.

Bradley unties the drawstring on his workout pants. Lets them fall to the floor. He's wearing a jock strap that leaves little to the imagination.

KEVIN: Wow.
BRADLEY: You like?
KEVIN: A lot.
BRADLEY: Come back over here.

Kevin goes into the kitchen. Looks for a place to stand where he'll be out of the way. There isn't a good spot. He hoists himself onto the counter. Watches as Bradley mops.

KEVIN: You're not judging me, are you?
BRADLEY: Why would I judge you?
KEVIN: The stuff about my dad. The fact that I tell people he's dead.
BRADLEY: Dude, that's self-preservation.
KEVIN: I guess.
BRADLEY: I'm not judging you.
KEVIN: Good.

Bradley mops some more. Then...

BRADLEY: If you want to touch yourself, you can. It's fine with me.
KEVIN: I want to touch *you*. Can I?

Some mopping. Then...

BRADLEY: That's forty more bucks on top of the other extra forty.
KEVIN: That's not a problem.

Bradley moves closer so he's standing in between Kevin's legs.

BRADLEY: You can use your hands, but no mouth. And I'm not going to touch you.

Kevin reaches down, grabs Bradley's bulge.

KEVIN: Sorry, this is—it's an awkward angle.
BRADLEY: Get off the counter.

Kevin hops off the counter.

KEVIN: Are you thirsty? I suddenly realized I never offered you anything—
BRADLEY: I'm good. Get back to what you started up there.

> *Kevin grabs Bradley's bulge again. Tugs at him through the jock strap.*

KEVIN: Can I take it out?

BRADLEY: Kevin? Look me in the eyes. Listen carefully. Hands good, mouth bad. You have my explicit consent to do whatever you want, as long as you follow those rules. So stop asking for my permission and get what you need.

KEVIN: Sorry—I just wanted to make sure I understood your parameters.

BRADLEY: Stop talking, Kevin.

> *Kevin pulls Bradley's jock strap down. He grabs Bradley's cock, stroking it.*

KEVIN: We should go where there's more—room.

BRADLEY: Good idea.

> *Neither one of them moves. Kevin just stands there, holding Bradley's dick.*

BRADLEY: I can't walk unless you let go.

KEVIN: Oh, yeah, okay, of course, sorry.

BRADLEY: Don't worry, you'll get it back in a few seconds.

They walk into the living room and sit on the bed. Bradley leans back, closes his eyes. Kevin touches himself through his pants as he aggressively strokes Bradley.

KEVIN: I fucking love your cock.
BRADLEY: Yeah?
KEVIN: Yeah.

Bradley grabs Kevin's hand.

BRADLEY: Hey hey hey—slow down.
KEVIN: Sorry.
BRADLEY: This is a marathon, not a sprint.
KEVIN: I get it.

Kevin resumes the handjob, taking more care.

KEVIN: Is that...?
BRADLEY: Yeah, that's better.

Kevin continues to stroke Bradley's cock. After a few beats, Kevin reaches over with his other hand...and tugs on Bradley's balls.

*Bradley closes his eyes,
leans back,
and lets out a
gentle
moan...*

Kevin gets into a nice, smooth rhythm.

Bradley looks at Kevin.
They lock eyes,
as Kevin strokes
and tugs.

This goes on for awhile.

It goes on longer than you expect it to.

It should get uncomfortable.

When I say "it should get uncomfortable," I don't mean for Kevin and Bradley.

They're together.
They're connecting.
Getting lost in the moment.

I mean: it should get uncomfortable for the audience. Watching this moment between two men. It should feel almost unbearably intimate.

Like, are we watching a play...
or are we watching a sex act?

When does a play called Handjob
become
an
actual
handjob?

At some point during the handjob, Kevin pulls his own cock out and begins to stroke himself too.

Until—

BRADLEY: Can we stop?

> *Kevin immediately pulls away from Bradley.*

KEVIN: Is everything okay?
BRADLEY: I feel uncomfortable. I need to stop.

> *Bradley grabs a pillow, covers himself.*

KEVIN: Do you want to go back?
BRADLEY: No, I don't want to go back. I want to talk through what we just did. It made me uncomfortable and I want—

> *Bradley looks out into the house.*

Susan? Susan, can we—

> *SUSAN appears in the aisle of the theater.*

| SUSAN: Jeffrey, can we— / what is the problem here? Because we need to finish the run-through, and I'd rather not stop— | BRADLEY/JEFFREY: No. I know what you're gonna— NO. I need to talk about what just happened. |

SUSAN: All right, everybody. You can both get [dressed] —

(*calling off, and motioning*)

Kate, can we get Jeffrey his [robe]? And can we save the lights?

> *The actor playing Kevin, who we will now refer to as TREVOR, buttons his pants back up.*

TREVOR: What just happened? What was that?

> *KATE, the ASM, dressed in black and wearing a headset, emerges with a terrycloth robe for the actor playing Bradley, who we will now refer to as JEFFREY.*

JEFFREY: You know what fucking happened.

> *Kate hands a bottle of Purell to Trevor, who cleans his hands. She exits into the wings.*

SUSAN: Let's talk about why you stopped.
TREVOR: Did I do something wrong?

SUSAN: What's the issue?

TREVOR: If you're upset about something—

JEFFREY: I am, actually. You're not supposed to take your dick out.

TREVOR: It felt like the right thing to do, in the moment.

JEFFREY: But it's not in the script—

TREVOR: I was following my instincts.

JEFFREY: No, it was self-indulgent.

TREVOR: It was *natural*.

JEFFREY: You decided—in the moment—to expose yourself, and you think that's natural?

TREVOR: I wasn't—*no*. I was playing the scene!

JEFFREY: More like hijacking the scene.

SUSAN: Okay, Jeffrey, I need you to dial it down a notch—

JEFFREY: Easy for you to say—I'm up here on this stage—

TREVOR: Yeah, with your dick out, so why can't my dick be out?

JEFFREY: Because of *what it says* in the script—it says you keep your dick in your fucking pants. It's an actual plot point!

TREVOR: The stage directions leave room for interpretation—

SUSAN: Are we really having / this argument right now?

JEFFREY: Give me a fucking break, Trevor.

TREVOR: They do, though!

JEFFREY: Did you pay *any* attention to all that table work we did? Kevin keeps it in his pants because he isn't comfortable with his body. Which feeds into the violence at the end of the play, when they beat each other up. It's all connected. Kevin uses his hands for a violent act because he can't allow himself to fully engage in the sensual one. We've talked about this endlessly! Look at the fucking text!

TREVOR: I was in the moment. It's *my* character.

JEFFREY (*to Susan*): Do you think it's okay that he did that?

SUSAN: I think there's room to explore.

JEFFREY: No. *Fuck* no!

SUSAN: Fuck yes! Jeffrey! This isn't a painting for fuck's sake. We have to listen to our instincts—

JEFFREY: No, this is one of those things that needs to be *set*. What does it say in the script?

Kate emerges with the script, hands it to Susan. She finds the right page.

SUSAN: "They walk into the living room. Bradley sits on the bed. Kevin sits next to him, still clothed. Bradley leans back, closes his eyes. Kevin puts his hand down his own pants as he reaches over and aggressively strokes Bradley's cock."

TREVOR: That feels like a jumping off point to me. As long as we're in that ballpark—

JEFFREY: Are you fucking kidding? As if we haven't spent weeks dissecting this scene.

TREVOR: Kevin's fucking jerking off! Who keeps their dick in their pants when they're jerking off?

JEFFREY: *Kevin* does!

TREVOR: How about you stop worrying about what my character does and focus on your own? Your stakes were so low tonight, it's like acting with a corpse.

(*poking Jeffrey in the stomach*)

Boop.
JEFFREY: No, fuck that.
SUSAN: Breathe.
JEFFREY: I don't want to breathe.
SUSAN: One deep, calming breath.
JEFFREY: No, listen to me—LISTEN—I need you to back me up here, Susan—
SUSAN: I'm listening.
JEFFREY: At this point in the play, do you think Kevin trusts Bradley?
SUSAN: They're still feeling each other out. This is the first time Kevin's paid for someone like you to clean his apartment. He's nervous. It's been a long time since Kevin's been close to anyone, sexually or otherwise. He's taking a risk, he's exposing himself emotionally.
JEFFREY: Which means the handjob is out of Kevin's comfort zone.
SUSAN: It's not your job to define Kevin's comfort zone.
TREVOR (*to Jeffrey*): Yeah, can you stop analyzing *my character* and admit it's out of *your* comfort zone?
JEFFREY: It *is*, actually.
TREVOR: Then fucking SAY THAT.

JEFFREY: I AM FUCKING SAYING THAT.

TREVOR: No, you're not, you're attacking me and my instincts.

JEFFREY: Because your instincts—no, your *choices*—crossed a fucking line! Why bother to choreograph all the sex stuff—SETTING it—if you're gonna throw it out the window?

TREVOR: It's called BEING IN THE MOMENT.

JEFFREY: No, it was "a choice." Wasn't it, Trevor? You chose to take your dick out.

TREVOR: It was a *choice* in the *moment,* which is an *instinct.*

JEFFREY: This is harassment.

TREVOR: Oh, come on!

SUSAN: Kate, can you give us the room?

JEFFREY: Do you hear me, Susan? It's fucking harassment.

SUSAN: You can't throw that word around lightly.

JEFFREY: Believe me, I DON'T. He harassed me.

TREVOR: Please don't start with the hashtag "Me Too" stuff.

JEFFREY: You're not on the Me Too train?

TREVOR: Of course I am. I support women. I believe women.

SUSAN: Thank you, Trevor.

TREVOR: But what I don't support is men trying to appropriate the progress women have made. Come up with your own hashtag.

JEFFREY: I don't care about a hashtag. I care about what you did to me. And I don't feel safe doing this play if you're gonna do things with your dick / that we didn't establish ahead of time.

SUSAN: Whoa, whoa, whoa—

You don't feel safe?

JEFFREY: I love the play. But if Trevor's gonna pull shit like that, then—

TREVOR: Oh *come on*. Dude! It's not like you have to touch it. I'm the one touching both the dicks! God, this is so messed up. You're thinking of quitting? We open on Saturday. Do you realize how unprofessional that is?

JEFFREY: No—don't put this on me.

TREVOR: I totally saw this coming, by the way, when I found out you were straight. I told them at the auditions—didn't I, Susan?

SUSAN: Yes, / you did.

TREVOR: I said: "*you need two gay actors.*" I told you! Aside from the issues of representation, you wouldn't have to deal with all this "straight panic" bullshit. We would've had a common language, we wouldn't have spent all that time talking about the culture of cruising, it would've been something the other actor *innately* understood. God, that would've been *heaven*. But this—this is a fucking nightmare. It really is, Susan. Susan, *Susan*.

SUSAN: I hear you.

TREVOR: It's fucking nuts, it's nightmare nonsense.

JEFFREY: This has nothing to do with my sexuality, Trevor.

TREVOR: Except a gay guy wouldn't say that.

JEFFREY: No, no, no: don't play the gay actor card—

TREVOR: I kind of have to, when you're being such a homophobe—

SUSAN: Okay, whoa, whoa, WHOA—

JEFFREY: I let you touch my dick, don't I?

SUSAN: Slow down.

TREVOR: You think letting a gay guy touch your dick in a play proves you aren't homophobic?

JEFFREY: Yes.

TREVOR: Your heterosexual privilege is stunning—

JEFFREY: Oh, *come on*—

SUSAN: Trevor—

TREVOR: I can't believe you don't see it. You don't even hear it. That's so fucking gross.

SUSAN: You guys—STOP.

TREVOR: I bet you go home to your girlfriend and brag about letting a fag play with your dick—

JEFFREY: I do, actually!

SUSAN: That's enough.

TREVOR: You use that word? You think that's your language?

SUSAN: We're getting off topic.

TREVOR: Answer the question.

SUSAN: If you're going to blow up my rehearsal, we need to at least try to have a civil discussion.

TREVOR: No. I want to know where we stand.

JEFFREY: Yes. I have the right to say that word.

TREVOR: *To say faggot.*

SUSAN: Guys—

JEFFREY: I have a gay uncle and a gay brother.

TREVOR: Oh, give me a fucking break.

JEFFREY: And I'm in a play where I get naked and receive a handjob from a gay guy. So yes: I can say fag if I want to say fag.

I'm basically a fag-by-proxy.

TREVOR: That doesn't even make sense. You're saying you can vote for gay people?

JEFFREY: You know what I mean: I'm an honorary faggot.

TREVOR: That isn't better—

JEFFREY: I'm fag-adjacent.

SUSAN: Guys—

TREVOR: Stop it—

JEFFREY: I'm fluent in fag.

SUSAN: *Guys*—

TREVOR: Stop saying that word! You don't have the right to say that word.

JEFFREY: *Fag*.

SUSAN: Okay, that's enough!

TREVOR (*to Susan*): Did you hear that?

JEFFREY: All I did was say the word—

TREVOR: It's *the way* you said it—

SUSAN: Stop! Both of you!

JEFFREY (*to Susan*): I don't understand why you're more upset about me saying a *word* than you are about Trevor just *taking his dick out of his pants*. Why aren't you more upset about that?

SUSAN: Jeffrey, I understand *you're* upset. I do. I hear you. But I'm the director, let me do my job.

JEFFREY: Then *do it*.

SUSAN: We've discussed boundaries. We spent hours of rehearsal time analyzing the text, coming at it clinically, so there wouldn't be surprises. We even brought in Liz for that intimacy training session—

JEFFREY: One session. *One* session!

SUSAN: Yes, a productive session that went very well—

JEFFREY: Clearly it didn't because Trevor took his dick out!

TREVOR: It was a motivated dick reveal.

JEFFREY: What does that even mean? No! Fuck! Liz should still be in the room, / she should be here *right now*—	SUSAN: Do you know how busy she is—

TREVOR: Liz was just a fancy choreographer. A choreographer choreographs, a director directs. / It's Susan's job now.

SUSAN: Exactly. Thank you. And I don't need an extra voice in the room making things muddy. Liz did her job—

TREVOR: Right, she gave us the tools we needed / for the scene—

JEFFREY: What fucking tools? She didn't give us any *language* to actually discuss when things got problematic—

SUSAN: The point is, Jeffrey, you *knew* penises coming out was the nature of this scene. So for you to stop a run and question Trevor's motivations: that's not your job. Did he go too far? Was it self-indulgent? / That's for me to decide.

JEFFREY: Those aren't the only options—

SUSAN: Let me finish. For you to say—and I don't mean to shame you—but for you to act surprised, to ask why I'm not upset? I'm sorry, Jeffrey, but that's mendacious of you.

JEFFREY: I don't know what that means.

SUSAN: I'm saying it feels dishonest.

JEFFREY: Were you watching that run-through just now? Did you see Trevor take his dick out when he explicitly *wasn't supposed to take his dick out? That's* the real issue here.

SUSAN: But he was able to do that / because—

TREVOR: To explore the moment—

SUSAN: Yes, thank you, he was able to explore the moment because we've created this safe space together—

JEFFREY: But I don't feel safe! How can this be a safe space if I don't feel safe?

SUSAN: I hear you. I'm sorry if I didn't hear you before. So tell me: why don't you feel safe?

JEFFREY: When we started the rehearsal process, you wanted us to be comfortable with each other. And you worked hard to make this, like you said, a safe space—

SUSAN: Thank you.

JEFFREY: But then Trevor took his dick out, and, well, that brings up a larger issue here—

TREVOR: No pun intended.

JEFFREY: Okay, no—don't do that—don't make a fucking dick joke—

SUSAN: Yeah, that's not helping, Trevor—

JEFFREY: What you were saying about safe spaces, Susan, it's like: we've made this space *too safe*. If Trevor feels "safe" enough to take his dick out when the script says he keeps it in his pants, then—anything can happen.

TREVOR: But that's what makes theater exciting: that sense of danger.

JEFFREY: There should be boundaries.

SUSAN: I want to push the audience. These are questions I want to explore. It's why I sparked to the script—

JEFFREY: I don't have a problem with the script.

TREVOR: You have a problem with my dick—

JEFFREY: That fucking pisses me off—

TREVOR: I can tell.

JEFFREY: For you to make light of the actual, real issue here—

TREVOR: *My dick.*

JEFFREY: It's more than that, actually. I let you guys bully me into thinking we were making an artistic statement, but what we're doing—this whole scene—

SUSAN: No, please do not backtrack on me / like this.

JEFFREY: It's too much! Jerking off on stage is too much, it's too far—

SUSAN: Jesus fucking Christ.

JEFFREY: The actual act. If an audience sees the body parts, if they see the act, that's all they're gonna see. And it's like, *where's the nuance*?

SUSAN: You want to talk about nuance?

JEFFREY: Yes! Nuance! All we're giving the audience is bodies—

SUSAN: That's not even remotely true.

JEFFREY: We're giving them dick, literally, and that's it: when you whip a dick out on-stage, it ruins the illusion of reality. It takes the audience out of the play—

SUSAN: You don't even hear how reductive that is.

JEFFREY: That's what I'm saying! Dicks are reductive! They're a distraction.

TREVOR: Except my dick's the distracting one. Isn't that what you said?

JEFFREY: No—I mean, yes, your dick was inappropriate because it wasn't supposed to come out *at all*—but now I'm saying: *all dicks*! All dicks are distracting. All dicks are a problem. All dicks!

SUSAN: Jesus fucking Christ.

JEFFREY: How do you think this scene's going to make people feel?

SUSAN: They might be uncomfortable, but I *want* that.

JEFFREY: Really?

SUSAN: Yes! I want them to confront their discomfort and come out the other side. If someone comes to something I've directed and the only reaction they have is "that was *nice*, what a *nice* play," shoot me in the head. I want—no, not want, I fucking *need*—to make people feel unsettled, disoriented. As a queer woman of color—

JEFFREY: Why are any of those distinctions relevant? Your sexuality, your gender, / your race—

SUSAN: No, don't come at me acting ignorant.

TREVOR: Yeah, that's a bad look, dude.

JEFFREY: I'm serious—

SUSAN: Point of view is everything. It's all we have! I'm up against three layers of privilege and it's fucking relevant. I haven't worked as hard as I've worked to make artistic compromises now. / And when I first read this play—

JEFFREY: It's not a compromise, it's theater etiquette—

SUSAN: Don't interrupt me. When I read the play, I asked myself: why do we need another play about two cis white men? We already have *the entire Western canon*. But what kept gnawing at me, what made me say yes, was the opportunity to create something sex positive and aggressively queer. It's an opportunity for me to subvert the system, using the tools that defined the system for so long. And you want to take that away from me?

JEFFREY: It's just, what if—couldn't we, like, stage it in a way that implies more, that's not as in your face, that's—

SUSAN: No! I'm not interested in playing it safe! The sanitized version of this play would be a hurtful lie. I *want* it to be *in your face*. People need to leave the theater and have *this* conversation. Let's elevate some heart rates. Let's wake people up! If we sanitize this scene, if we	TREVOR: Yes! Fucking yesssss!

stage it in a neutered way, then we're back to "what a nice, nice play." If all we can make is a "nice play," what the fuck are we even doing here? Let's force people to confront their boundaries, their biases. Let's incite some actual goddamn emotion. Get them arguing at the bar afterwards about whether any of this was even necessary.

Amen.

JEFFREY: What if people walk out?

SUSAN: Then fucking let them!

JEFFREY: Okay, but—aren't you worried about triggering people, people who've been abused, for example. Forcing them to watch a sex act, it could re-traumatize a person—

SUSAN: *The play is called Handjob*, for fuck's sake. The faint of heart didn't get this far. We aren't tricking anyone, or taking advantage. Besides, they saw the "mature audiences" warning on the website, on the poster, on our Instagram—and they still bought tickets.

JEFFREY: You're taking advantage of me then. I know I said I'd be naked, but it feels wrong now, the way things have gone—

TREVOR: Jesus, we open on Saturday and suddenly you're shy?

JEFFREY: It's not the nudity—it's how we use the nudity. I mean, does something have to be real to be truthful? Why does the audience have to see the act? Shouldn't there be a line—some sort of level of decency—that we don't cross?

SUSAN: All these questions you're asking: that's all in the play! When was the last time you went to a theater and really lost yourself? The first time I saw a Sarah Kane play, I literally didn't breathe until it was over; it was visceral, violent, / graphic.

JEFFREY: Who?

SUSAN: Sarah Kane made me *think* in a different way. You don't know who Sarah Kane is?

JEFFREY: No.

SUSAN: They called *Blasted* "disgusting," "filthy." This might be an apocryphal story but I think I read somewhere that *The Guardian* critic threw up in the stalls on opening night. And the amazing thing is—all this hostility, this vitriol—it wasn't misguided. Kane wanted that reaction: she showed us the atrocities of war, and forced us not to look away. One character rapes this soldier, then eats his eyeballs, and / then later—

JEFFREY (*disgusted*): Oh *god*.   TREVOR (*thrilled*):
                                        Oh. *GOD*.

SUSAN: —he's been obliterated by this war, he has nothing, he's beyond his breaking point and I—I still see it, I still feel the horror—he literally eats a dead baby, and—

JEFFREY: And you enjoyed that?

SUSAN: I'm trying to explain the effect it had on me. A part of my brain knew it was theater, but then ANOTHER PART believed everything on that stage, BELIEVED what I was seeing. It wasn't real; it was the truth. I left my body. All that was left was the experience of the play and the reality it created in me. I saw him do the worst imaginable thing someone could do, and yet: I felt for him. *I felt for him.* That's why I do this: so we can create moments like that. Moments of extreme empathy.

TREVOR: Incredible.

JEFFREY: But what we're dealing with here isn't about violence, it's about touching.

SUSAN: You didn't hear anything I just said.

JEFFREY: I did! But we've gone off the rails. Sometimes we'll be running it, and it's like: one minute I'm *rehearsing* a play called *Handjob*, and then *I'm just getting a handjob.*

SUSAN: Yes. Yes! That's our "eating the dead baby" moment.

JEFFREY: What are you even—no! That's not [what I fucking meant] —I completely lose the character, it's just *me* on stage getting jacked off. Don't you see how fucked up that is?

SUSAN: It's what we're *striving* for!

JEFFREY: No—

SUSAN: Yes! Authenticity. The truth of the moment!

TREVOR: I taught this high school acting workshop a few weeks ago and I gave them scenes to work on from *Beyond Therapy*—

JEFFREY: How is this even remotely relevant?

TREVOR: If you'll let me finish / the story—

SUSAN: Let him finish, Jeffrey.

TREVOR: And these two students refused to do the scene because a character says "cocksucker." They were worried about offending someone. I asked, "Are you offended?" They said, "No, but other people might be." So instead of *doing the work* and finding the truth of the scene, they CENSORED THEMSELVES. This was Durang for fuck's sake, and they wouldn't even / read the scene out loud—

JEFFREY: Again, how is this relevant?

TREVOR: It's relevant because we're living in a culture of fear right now and it's suffocating artists, queer artists especially. It's silencing the truth-tellers and / I think that's—

JEFFREY (*disdain*): "*Truth-tellers.*"

TREVOR: —where *you're* coming from with this outburst, from that same place of fear. Don't you see how dangerous that is? If we let other people dictate the stories we can tell—

JEFFREY: Excuse me? Hello? We've lost sight of the fact that you violated me.

TREVOR: Not in the context of the scene!

JEFFREY: You exposed yourself! You violated me—and if you did that in front of an audience, you'd be violating them too.

TREVOR: That's horseshit.

SUSAN: If you jerk off in a hotel room, in front of the maid—*that's* a violation. But if you put it on-stage—if you *light* it for Christ's sake—then there's artistic intent. And that's what we're doing here. People are buying tickets. That's an act of consent.

JEFFREY: That's so fucking bogus.

SUSAN: This play is a conversation, and when someone buys a ticket they're telling us they want to be part of that conversation.

JEFFREY: The truth is, all you're gonna get is an audience of gay guys who want to see naked men.

SUSAN: So you're reducing / what I said to ticket sales.

TREVOR: What's wrong with a gay audience?

JEFFREY: Nothing. It's just—I mean, look, no offense, but...

TREVOR: Too late.

JEFFREY: ...there's a lot of creepy gay guys out there. / And those are the guys—

TREVOR: Wow.

JEFFREY: —who are gonna come see this show. They're gonna come for the wrong reasons.

TREVOR: Stop talking.

JEFFREY: You know I'm right.

TREVOR: You're talking about me, you know. I'm that gay audience. Who would see this play? *This fag*. And maybe I'd go for the wrong reasons. Maybe I'd go because the guy on the poster was hot, and I heard there was real sex on stage, and it's titillating. Let's say that's why I came here: to get turned on. What the hell's wrong with that? You think guys are gonna get *so* confused by what's happening on stage? You think they'll forget where they are and turn the theater into an all-out fuck-fest sex club?

JEFFREY: No.

TREVOR: Is that what you think of us? Of me? Is it?

JEFFREY: No.

TREVOR: You sure about that?

JEFFREY: Look, I did fucking Shakespeare in the Park last summer, okay? Ben Brantley said we reinvented *Merchant*. And I chose to do this play, so obviously I saw something in it—

TREVOR: You were a torchbearer.

JEFFREY: I was still on-stage with John motherfucking Goodman!

TREVOR: *As a torchbearer.*

JEFFREY: What I'm saying is, I went from that to getting a handjob, and it's like: can't we give the audience more than a handjob? Because if it's *just* sex, it isn't art.

SUSAN: It isn't just sex for the sake of sex. It's relevant to the story we're telling—

JEFFREY: What story is that, exactly? Why is it so important to stage it this way? To go this far?

SUSAN: Oh, you want me to defend this moment? After how many weeks of rehearsal, after how many conversations—you're asking me to do that. Again.

JEFFREY: Yes.

SUSAN: Fine. The play's about intimacy.

Beat.

JEFFREY: ...and?

> *Keith has entered the back of the theater. He stands and listens. Unseen by the others.*

SUSAN: We meet this man, Kevin, who's lonely. He spends his days at a computer. He doesn't take care of himself, physically or emotionally. We see this represented in the apartment, his environment—there's a level of filth there. Filth is perhaps too strong a word, but the point is: his exterior matches his interior. Then he hires Bradley, this *stranger*, to perform a cleansing, an ablution. Ultimately the act of cleaning is secondary: what Kevin's paying for is companionship. Later in the play, we discover he's still reeling from an unexpected death, the loss of his husband. Kevin's in mourning. But we don't know that in the handjob scene, which is why it works best if it's raw, open, literally naked. All we see is two men fulfilling a need. But when we have all the puzzle pieces, we look back and see how Kevin's fumbling, how he's trying to put his life back together. We realize how far gone he is, how much he's lost. We see pathos, desperation, yearning. But it's hopeful, too, because: he's *trying*, he's dusting off the pictures of his former life, moving forward. The audience is left to consider how a person emerges from loss, how you rebuild a life. The central act of the play is an act of touching. Not being touched: *touching*. Kevin's reconnecting with his sexuality, it's a restorative moment. I'd argue that it saves him. But ultimately I want the audience to decide. Kevin

may be reborn, but at what cost?
JEFFREY: Okay. I get all that. But the bottom line is: as soon as the audience sees a naked body, their minds shut off. When people are confronted with nudity, it's all they see.
KEITH: I think maybe I should be part of this conversation.

Keith comes out on stage.

SUSAN: Keith! Do you think what we're doing up here—the way we're doing it—do you think it's pornographic?
JEFFREY: Hold up, that's not my main cause of concern—
TREVOR: Jesus, make up your mind—
SUSAN: Now wait just a minute, Jeffrey—because I want to make sure this is clear—did you or did you not just say you have a problem with the graphic nature of the scene?
JEFFREY: Yes, that's *part* of what I said, / but—
TREVOR: It's what you said, dude. It's why you stopped the run-through: because you don't want to be naked in the scene—
JEFFREY: That's not even remotely what happened tonight—
SUSAN: Stop it, both of you. Keith, answer the question, please.
KEITH: I wouldn't use the word "pornographic."
JEFFREY: Of course you wouldn't.
SUSAN: Let him speak!
JEFFREY: He can't see it impartially.
KEITH: But I can speak to intention. And what I'm trying to capture with this scene is: a vulnerable moment between two men. It's

important to show that.

JEFFREY: Except I don't think we need to *see* it.

KEITH: Why not?

JEFFREY: Because it's too far.

KEITH: I completely disagree.

JEFFREY: It feels like exploitation.

KEITH: No, we've got too many hang-ups about sex in this country—

JEFFREY: Before you go on a tangent about our nation's sexual hang-ups, there's something that happened tonight that you should know about—

TREVOR: It was a real moment.

KEITH: Okay, let me finish this thought: that moment between Kevin and Bradley—it's a true, honest, genuine moment. I'm not gonna shy away from that.

JEFFREY: But what if we staged it differently, like if we angled the bed in a certain way—

SUSAN: That's not gonna happen.

KEITH: I think it's essential to depict that moment graphically. Visually. Fully. We don't see enough positive depictions of gay men—

JEFFREY: Do you honestly think this is a positive portrayal of gay men?

KEITH: I do.

JEFFREY: It's a cheap sexual encounter. An aggressive handjob—

KEITH: Why do you think it's cheap?

JEFFREY: Because they aren't going to see each other the next day!

SUSAN: We don't know that, Jeffrey. The ending's ambiguous.

JEFFREY: They *beat each other up*. Don't tell me that's a happy ending—

KEITH: Kevin and Bradley have a moment. An afternoon. It ends badly, but before it takes a turn, they have a brief connection. And that connection is elegant, / substantial, —

JEFFREY: Elegant?

KEITH: —beautiful even. The fact that it's ephemeral doesn't make the moment "less than." It's important to give the moment weight. To depict it without holding back, or shying away.	SUSAN: Yes. *Mmhmm.* Yes, yes.

JEFFREY: That's such liberal pansy bullshit. I'm progressive, I'm open, I'm sex-positive...but there's some things I don't want to *see*, and one of those things is a real, unfaked handjob. I'd bet most of our potential audience feels the same way.

TREVOR: All the gay people, you mean? Since they're the only people who are gonna come see this play. Isn't that what you said?

JEFFREY: Don't twist my words—

KEITH: People get shot every day in this country and we don't do anything to stop it—

JEFFREY: That doesn't have *anything* to do with what we're talking about.

KEITH: It has everything to do with the images we choose to put out into the world. This moment in the play, it's not about shame—it's about a man who needs to be touched and another man who's there for him—

JEFFREY: But Kevin doesn't get *touched*. He's the one *touching*. And since we're talking / about that moment, you should know—

KEITH: The details aren't important: he gets what he can within the parameters he's given. It's about the connection. If we stage it in a way that implies they have something to hide, then we're saying it's shameful. It's a way of pussyfooting around what they're doing, it says to the audience: *"we don't think you can handle seeing two men having a tender moment."* But we have mass shootings in this country nearly every day, and they put it in front of our fucking faces relentlessly. These preventable, communal tragedies, yet nothing changes. *That's* where we should focus our shame. Instead, we're complacent, and the culture we consume gets more violent—and we're conditioned to accept this violence. So when we see it on screen or on stage, we don't flinch, we ACCEPT it. And with sex—we're still so damned terrified of depicting this essential part of our lives. Why do we have to shy away from showing an intimate moment between two men? Why can't it be a casual, normal thing to depict? Even if it's only, like you said, a *hookup*.

JEFFREY: Okay, but what happened in the run-through brings up issues of consent.

KEITH: That's not what the scene's about—

JEFFREY: I know, but—

KEITH: It's about connection. Which we so desperately need! We live in this world that keeps inventing new ways to keep us apart—we spend all our time staring at screens—so when two people seek each other out—when they have a real, honest interaction like they do in this scene—that's a beautiful thing. Why can't I depict that? Why do I, as an artist, have to be afraid of that? Because there are still people who find it disgusting? Who find me disgusting? Do *you* find it disgusting?

JEFFREY: No. That's not my issue here—

KEITH: Give me a moment between two consenting, adult men. Show me what that looks like. Because that's my experience in the world—but I don't see it. And don't you fucking dare say: "But you have *Brokeback,* you have *Moonlight*, you have *Angels in America*." As if that's enough. I get a handful of queer stories in the mainstream media a year, and you get hundreds, thousands, endless pieces of entertainment to see yourself in. I remember when I was a young gay—and by "young gay" I mean twenty-seven, because I was a "late gay" too—I used to flip through the channels on my TV at night and play this game where I wouldn't settle on a show until I found one with a gay character, someone I saw myself in. Some nights, I'd flip through channels for hours. Click, click, click, click, click. So I look out at the world and that's the absence I see, and the thing that fills that absence is all the carnage. The never-ending cycle of shootings and "thoughts and prayers." Every decrepit conservative degenerate in the GOP is entrenched in this putrid, soul-sucking way of life, falling over themselves to suck the NRA's hard metallic cock. This myth they've created, this notion of a *"good guy with a gun"* —*that's* pornographic, *that's* exploitation. *That* makes me uncomfortable. It's a nightmare. *It's ugly*. But this scene between two men? Where is the harm in that? Really, truly: where is the harm? You toss around the word pornographic, you fear we might go too far, but: it's just a dick. It shouldn't make you uncomfortable. And I judge you if it does. *I judge you*. So yes, fine, we all have a "line" in the sand. We all have our own idea of "too far." But stop worrying about what's too far: we're depicting an intimate act between two men. If that's *crossing a line,* then cross that line. Fucking cross it. Normalize it. You shouldn't be afraid of a guy touching another guy's dick. I want to see more men enjoying their dicks together on stage, God-fucking-damn-it. It doesn't require a debate: it's just a dick. Touch the dick and move on to the next scene. Okay?

Beat.

TREVOR: That's basically what I've been saying.
SUSAN: I think we should stop talking, take a break, then get back to
    work. Kate, can you reset the props?

Kate enters and gets to work. Everyone else begins to disperse. Jeffrey looks shell-shocked.

And then...

KATE: It's two dicks.

Everyone stops.

KEITH: What?

JEFFREY: Yeah. That's right! *It's two dicks.*

TREVOR: Are you having a stroke?

JEFFREY: Keith said "it's just a dick."

KEITH: So?

JEFFREY: You said it shouldn't make me uncomfortable.

KEITH: It shouldn't.

JEFFREY: All I'm trying to say is—it's not just my dick we're talking about, *it's two dicks—*

TREVOR: Oh God, are we really gonna hash through all that again? You're making me hate theater.

SUSAN: Yeah, this isn't productive anymore.

JEFFREY: You know what, maybe you were right, maybe you guys *should* have hired a gay actor. Maybe you wouldn't have railroaded him—

TREVOR: Can't we just run through the scene and see what happens?

JEFFREY: Not until we're done talking this through.

Don't you even care, Keith?

Don't you want to know the actual violation that happened while we were rehearsing *your* play? The violation to my body? Or are we gonna pretend the real issue here is gun violence?

Beat.

KEITH: What happened to you?
JEFFREY: We choreographed the scene. The scene was set. And then Trevor exposed himself to me.
KEITH: That's all?
JEFFREY: You don't think that's an issue?
KEITH: I think we need to finish the run-through.
JEFFREY: And *I* think I need to know if Trevor's gonna take his dick out again.
SUSAN (*taking the reigns*): You know what, Jeffrey, we'll do the scene how we do the scene. You've been driving the car your whole life. It's time for you to sit in the passenger seat. Let's set the stage for the top of Five.

Lights fade.

SCENE FIVE

Keith's apartment.

Keith is at the door with Eddie.

KEITH: I'm sorry the place is a mess. I've been meaning to clean.

EDDIE: You say that every month.

KEITH: I know, but usually I tidy up a little bit before you get here.

EDDIE: Do you really?

KEITH: A little.

EDDIE: That's a lie and you know it. But you do you, man.

KEITH: I feel like I could learn a lot from you about "doing me."

EDDIE: Is that some sort of come on?

KEITH: Oh, no—God, no—I'm saying you're confident. You really know how to "do you." And I feel like I could learn from that.

EDDIE: Because I'm a heterosexual black man who doesn't have a problem taking his shirt off and cleaning in front of gay men for money? That's what you mean?

KEITH: Yes. That.

Also, you should know I don't think of you as black.

EDDIE: What's that supposed to mean?

KEITH: You described yourself as a "heterosexual black man" and I wanted to point out that I don't think of you as black. I don't have you labeled that way.

EDDIE: How do you have me "labeled?"

KEITH: Just...you know. Eddie. Cleaner.

EDDIE: "Cleaner."

KEITH: That's literally how I have you listed in my phone: Eddie Cleaner. You haven't told me your last name and I never wanted to pry. But it's an appropriate label, right? Because it's what you do.

EDDIE: That's how you see me?

KEITH: Is that wrong?

EDDIE: It's illuminating, actually.

KEITH: Okay, well...could you start with the kitchen today?

EDDIE: Are you really not gonna say anything?

KEITH: I don't know what you mean.

EDDIE: You're never gonna say the words, are you? That fucking blows my mind.

KEITH: Is something...? Is something wrong?

EDDIE: I am AMAZED by your fuckitude.

KEITH: What's going on? What's with this hostility?

EDDIE: I can't believe this shit—you're actually playing dumb. *God give me the strength.*

KEITH: Can you please tell me what you're upset about? If something's wrong...

EDDIE: I saw your play.

KEITH: Which one?

EDDIE: "*Which one?*" As if you're Edward Albee.

KEITH: You saw *Handjob*.

EDDIE: I was there last night.

KEITH: I'm getting the impression you didn't enjoy yourself.

EDDIE: I didn't.

KEITH: That's okay, art's subjective.

EDDIE: I didn't like it *at all*.

KEITH: It isn't for everyone. And we had to replace a difficult actor at the last minute, so they're still finding their way.

EDDIE: If I can be blunt...

KEITH: Of course. I can take it.

EDDIE: I thought it was a piece of shit, actually.

KEITH: Oh. *Jesus*. That's. Wow.

EDDIE: It made me physically ill.

KEITH: Don't hold back.

EDDIE: You said you could take it.

KEITH: But you don't have to be *mean*.

EDDIE: You stole my story, dude.

KEITH: What are you talking about?

EDDIE: You stole my story and then you erased me.

KEITH: You think...my play...

EDDIE: It's *about me*.

KEITH: It's not.

EDDIE: Come on, man.

KEITH: I see how you might get that *impression*, but—it's not. The play. It's not about you.

EDDIE: *It is*, though.

KEITH: There's a shirtless cleaner, but that's where the similarities end.

EDDIE: You changed stuff, sure. But it was inspired by me. Things I've said to you, things I've told you in confidence—
KEITH: I swear Bradley isn't you.
EDDIE: You even gave him a name that sounds like mine! Eddie. Bradley. Eddie. Bradley.
KEITH: That wasn't a conscious choice. It's a coincidence! He's not you. Not exactly, at least.
EDDIE: *Not exactly*.
KEITH: He's more of an amalgam of several people I've met—
EDDIE: You're right: he isn't *exactly* me. Not the way you cast it.
KEITH: You didn't like the actor? That's what this is [about] —
EDDIE: Don't be dense, dude.
KEITH: You think this is a racial thing?
EDDIE: You don't?
KEITH: We tried to get a diverse cast.
EDDIE: Then you didn't try hard enough.
KEITH: *We tried*. We had several rounds of auditions. We saw hundreds of people.
EDDIE: "Hundreds."
KEITH: But what you have to understand is that a lot of people turned us down because of the explicit nature of the material.
EDDIE: Which was completely gratuitous, by the way—
KEITH: Actually—
EDDIE: I don't need to see a guy touch another guy's dick to know what a guy touching another guy's dick looks like. Don't show me that shit.

KEITH: Okay, that's a whole other discussion—

EDDIE: I almost fucking walked out.

KEITH: Anyway, that's beside the point, really, and—back to your original grievance: at the end of the day, we went with the best actors.

EDDIE: People like you always say that.

KEITH: We really did try—

EDDIE: If you tried hard enough to get a diverse cast, you would've had a diverse cast.

KEITH: Are you a casting director?

EDDIE: No.

KEITH: Then you don't know what it's like.

EDDIE: I know bullshit when I hear it.

KEITH: I don't think you fully grasp what goes into putting on a piece of theater—

EDDIE: I've got friends who could act circles around that guy in your play.

KEITH: We can't just hire some random guy. There's a process—

EDDIE: You think I don't know actors? Half of the guys I Crossfit with dance on Broadway.

KEITH: Look, we considered a person of color—

EDDIE: A black guy. Specifically.

KEITH: Yes. I'm saying, we were open. But—

EDDIE: But *what*? Stop trying to justify a bad decision with a shitty excuse.

KEITH: I'm not racist. I make theater.

EDDIE: As if one of those statements proves the other. Do you hear how idiotic that sounds?

KEITH: I'm telling you: I'm liberal, I'm open. I'm gay for fuck's sake!

EDDIE: *I'm not homophobic. I like pecan pies.*

KEITH: That's not—what's that even—

EDDIE: *I'm not homophobic. I'm double-jointed.*

KEITH: Why are you—

EDDIE: *I'm not homophobic. I went to a Carly Rae Jepsen concert once.*

KEITH: Stop saying absurd things.

EDDIE: So you hear how it sounds. How inane it sounds when you say you aren't racist "because you make theater?" How the two things have nothing to do with each other?

KEITH: Yes—no—I don't—look, you're getting me flustered. You can't call me racist—I'm not.

EDDIE: Best case scenario: you're lazy. Was the first actor black?

KEITH: What do you mean?

EDDIE: What do I fucking mean? You said you had to replace one of the actors—was it the cleaner?

KEITH: Yes.

EDDIE: And that first actor, was he a man of color?

KEITH: No.

EDDIE: So you made the wrong choice twice. Which means we're out of "best case scenario" territory. This wasn't a lazy move. This was more than that—

KEITH: I don't like how you're misrepresenting me right now—

EDDIE: Join the club.

KEITH: Can we talk about this without the anger?

EDDIE: You think this is anger? Jesus. I'm not angry. I choose not to waste my time like that. What I am is: *frustrated*. I am *frustrated* by your narrow view of the world.

KEITH: I'm frustrated too, then. Me too! So what if we—hypothetically—what if we pretend I hadn't cast my play yet. Pretend I'm still writing it. What could I have done better?

EDDIE: No, I'm not doing that.

KEITH: You don't want to help me understand?

EDDIE: I don't want to teach you. I don't want to *have to* teach you.

KEITH: But I want to know how I could've handled the whole situation better. I'm asking you—

EDDIE: That's not my job, dude. Use Google. Figure that shit out yourself.

KEITH: But don't you see that I'm actually—I'm trying here? And I'm glad you brought this up. It's just—I'm trying to figure out how to say this, but—there's a part of me that knew—that *knows*—that I handled this situation badly. There's a part of me that—okay, this is what I'm trying to say—the truth is: I kept hiring you so I could get to know you better. To understand the character.

EDDIE: You don't even hear how offensive that is.

KEITH: How is that offensive?

EDDIE: The fact that you don't see it—that you don't know—

KEITH: I'm trying—

EDDIE: That you claim the character isn't me, then say you kept hiring me so you could understand the character better. Don't you hear what a mind-fuck that is?

KEITH: Like I said, he's an amalgam of you and a few other people.

EDDIE: Amalgam my fucking ass.

KEITH: I don't know how to say it better.

EDDIE: No worries, I get it: you won't own up to shit. But I'm not gonna let you gaslight me.

KEITH: Look, maybe we could've tried harder to find a black guy, but—

EDDIE: But, but, but.

KEITH: But the play isn't—

EDDIE: But *what*?

KEITH: It isn't, ultimately, about race—

EDDIE: There it is...

KEITH: —so we ended up going a different direction.

EDDIE: ...another excuse.

KEITH: It's not an excuse. I'm telling you what happened.

EDDIE: Dude, that character in your play is *me*. Maybe you don't "label" me in a certain way—

KEITH: I know you're black. I'm aware. I'm not blind.

EDDIE: *Now* you notice. *Now* you're aware.

KEITH: But there's more to you than that—

EDDIE: You're gonna tell me all the things you know about me now? That's what's happening here?

KEITH: No, I'm saying: I'm *glad* you see yourself in the character. I wanted him to be universal—

EDDIE: Which is white.

KEITH: No. You aren't listening. That's not what I—no. The universality of the character, that's what you're ultimately responding to. I try to find inspiration all over the place, and I use all of it, I put all of it into the piece. All these little kernels that make up the whole. And this play—I was writing a gay play. That's what I wanted to focus on. And so, I didn't want—I don't know how to say this without you misinterpreting what I mean.

EDDIE: You didn't want the blackness of me getting in the way of the gayness of you.

KEITH: Something like that.

EDDIE: Jesus Christ.

KEITH: I'm just being honest.

EDDIE: Got it. Great. So we're playing the diversity Olympics.

KEITH: No—

EDDIE: And you're saying a white faggot has it harder than a straight nigger.

KEITH: What? Fuck no. No! I'm not saying that. I would *never* say that—

EDDIE: Admit it, Keith.

KEITH: I would never use those words.

EDDIE: I saw your play. You like to provoke.

KEITH: That's what *you're* doing right now. You're trying to provoke me. And I don't know why you're coming at me so hard—

EDDIE: Because you used me: the way I behave, the way I talk. You even used my uncle's coming out story, but you warped it, you turned it into this aria of victimhood—you used my stories, then you erased me. And now you belittle me, you—

KEITH: How did I belittle you?

EDDIE: You just called me a little kernel. You said that's all I was. A small part of the whole.

KEITH: Eddie, I can tell you're angry, but—

EDDIE: I already told you, dude, *this* is not anger. I'm actually starting to get you. You were scared to write something real.

KEITH: No.

EDDIE: You were, though. You didn't know how to get it right. You were afraid.

KEITH: Will you please stop mischaracterizing me?

EDDIE: Fine. Characterize yourself. If you weren't afraid, then what were you?

KEITH: I was *sensitive* to the fact that if I got the racial stuff wrong, it would be a big deal.

EDDIE: So you took the easy way out.

KEITH: No—

EDDIE: Yes, you did. But it's cool: I get it. *I get you.*

KEITH: I wouldn't call my play "easy" —

EDDIE: Did you ever think about what I really do? When I'm not cleaning?

KEITH: Of course I did.

EDDIE: No, you like to think of me cleaning. That's how you like to see me, isn't it?

KEITH: Not in a "looking down on you" way, if that's what you're implying.

EDDIE: I'm not naive, Keith. I know you get off on this. The power dynamic. The subjugation. Watching the black man clean. That turns you on.

KEITH: That isn't fair—

EDDIE: You groped me before.

KEITH: I apologized.

EDDIE: It still happened.

KEITH: I'm sorry.

EDDIE: You still haven't asked me what I do outside of all this.

KEITH: Okay, so...what do you—what else do you do?

EDDIE: I'm working on a PhD in Molecular, Cellular, and Evolutionary Biology.

KEITH: Wow. That's...I never met anyone who—that's—it's impressive, wow.

EDDIE: I'm kidding, dude.

KEITH: What do you mean?

EDDIE: I'm a playwright. That's the irony here. I'm in my second year at Juilliard.

KEITH: Are you serious?

EDDIE: Dead serious. This job? I've got a nice body and I'm good at cleaning, so I figured why not pay some bills? You were one of my first clients. But after doing this awhile, I started meeting interesting people. It became more than a job. It became research.

KEITH: You mean...

EDDIE: You wrote my play.

I was writing a play about my life story, then you stole it from me.

KEITH: Oh my God. I'm—holy shit. I'm sorry. I—I—I don't even know what to say. These things happen, though. Like that time there were two volcano movies. People get inspired by the same things. But this is—wow. Maybe there's a different angle you could use—

EDDIE: You used my angle.

KEITH: But everyone has their own voice, right? I mean, what is it they say? There's only, like, seven stories and we all, you know, tell them differently. Something like that. How far did you get? Do you want to pitch me your take on the story? There has to be some way to make it new again. What if—

EDDIE: Dude. I'm fucking with you.

KEITH: Wait, what?

EDDIE: This isn't Tiny Town, USA.

KEITH: You're—you're not a playwright?

EDDIE: No, I'm not your little poetic coincidence.

KEITH: Can you please be straight with me? For, like, five minutes. What is the truth?

EDDIE: The interesting thing is—and by "interesting," I mean completely pathetic and predictable—you believed the playwriting thing more easily than you believed the Molecular,

Cellular, and Evolutionary Biology thing. Which is true, by the way. But that doesn't jive with this image you have of me in your head, does it?

KEITH: No. It doesn't fit my image of you.

EDDIE: You don't look at me and see "scientist."

KEITH: I know you as a "cleaner." *That's how I know you.*

EDDIE: Then I'm glad you didn't try to represent me. Because you've got a shitty imagination—

KEITH: That's not true—

EDDIE: And besides, I'm tired of hearing stories from people like you. By the way, that play of yours? That jerk-off fantasy? You really think it's more interesting than what actually happened between the two of us?

KEITH: What actually happened?

EDDIE: You violated me. You groped me.

KEITH: I wouldn't call it that.

EDDIE: What would you call it?

KEITH: A mistake.

EDDIE: I've never mistakenly grabbed someone's crotch. That's not an accident, and it's not a mistake. It's a choice.

KEITH: I said I was sorry.

EDDIE: Fuck "sorry." I need more than "sorry." You touch me like that and I'm supposed to accept an apology and let it go?

KEITH: That was such a long time ago. You've been back here to clean—

EDDIE: That doesn't matter—

KEITH: It does, though. How many times have you been back? And you've been fine—

EDDIE: I thought I let it go. But I'm always aware you did that to me. That you're a guy who crossed that line. I'm a man. That shit's not supposed to bother me, right? Then I saw your play and realized it wasn't even something you were wrestling with. It's been eating away at me, but it made zero impression on you.

KEITH: That's not true.

EDDIE: You turned it into this other thing. Where the character *based on me* is complicit. He seeks out your touch, he gets you to give him money for it—he *wants* it. See, your play made me realize how differently you and I experienced that moment. *I* was ashamed. But *you* wrote a "piece of theater." When you're the one who should be ashamed. I need you to feel that. I need you to understand how your actions affect people. You don't get to say sorry and move on.

Beat.

I'm writing an essay.

KEITH: You said you weren't a writer.

EDDIE: I think I can handle an essay about the playwright who groped, then whitewashed me. The playwright who dehumanized me, then erased me. The playwright who took me out of his narrative. I'm thinking I'll submit it to Buzzfeed. I know a guy over there.

KEITH: Please don't do that.

EDDIE (*taking out his phone*): You're right, why wait? I could just tweet it out right now.

KEITH: Don't—

EDDIE: Have you ever seen something like this go viral? How quickly these things spread?

KEITH: Put your phone away.

EDDIE: You don't get to tell me what to do.

KEITH: I'm a good guy.

EDDIE: Good guys aren't always right.

KEITH: I misread the situation.

EDDIE: And I don't think you're as "good" as you think you are.

KEITH: It was a misunderstanding.

EDDIE: That doesn't make it okay.

KEITH: I've never done anything like that before.

EDDIE: That doesn't make it okay either.

KEITH: I won't do it again.

EDDIE: Still not okay.

KEITH: People will think I'm racist—they'll think I'm a harasser. That's not who I am. It was just a moment. But if people read about it—it's gonna define me—it's gonna—

EDDIE: I don't have control over what people think.

KEITH: They're gonna think that, though. And that's gonna stick to me—

EDDIE: All I'm writing is the truth.

KEITH: You don't have to do this. I said I was sorry. Don't do this—

EDDIE: You think I'm crossing a line?

KEITH: I do.

EDDIE: How's it feel?

KEITH: Fucked.

EDDIE: Yeah?

KEITH: Yes. I feel fucked.

EDDIE: Good. Maybe you'll remember how it feels next time you cross that line.

Eddie heads for the door.

KEITH: No, don't leave.

Keith grabs his arm.

EDDIE: Get your hands off me—

KEITH: We have to finish talking this through.

Keith tries to block the door.

EDDIE: Oh, is this how we're gonna do it?

Eddie shoves Keith.

KEITH: Come on. If you're mad at me, let out your aggression, whatever. I give you consent to hit me.

EDDIE: Dude.

Eddie steps away.

KEITH: Whatever you have to do.

EDDIE: You want me to beat you up like at the end of your play? Is that what's happening? You didn't earn that shit, and I'm not taking the bait. Step the fuck aside.

KEITH: No. I'm not letting you leave. We're not done here.

EDDIE: Come on, man—have some fucking dignity.

KEITH: I know, I know—but please—please don't—can you—can you just not use the word "grope?"

EDDIE: Do you know how pathetic you are?

KEITH: Write what you need but don't use that word. Please—

EDDIE: Can you see yourself?

KEITH: Can you just give me that one thing? Don't use the word. Otherwise I'm not moving. You'll have to push me out of the way. PUSH me out of the FUCKING way.

EDDIE: I'm not gonna fucking touch you.

KEITH: But if we keep talking—

EDDIE: There isn't anything else you can say to me, Keith.

KEITH: But if we come to an understanding—something between you and me—maybe you won't feel the need to write anything.

EDDIE: Nice try.

KEITH: I fucked up. I get it. But you don't need to punish me. Please.

EDDIE: You wrote your version of the story, now it's my turn.

KEITH: It's wrong. Your version is wrong.

EDDIE: You can write about that in your next play. I'm done talking to you.

KEITH: Wait—

> *He takes out some cash. Holds it out to Eddie.*

KEITH: Your rate, plus the tip. Take it.

EDDIE: I'm not even going to dignify that with a response.

> *Eddie exits without the money.*
>
> *Keith doesn't know what to do with himself. He stands at the door for a beat.*
>
> [Am I a racist? Did I harass him? Am I a bad person? Did I steal Eddie's story? Why did I grab him the first time we met? There was a sign, wasn't there? He gave me a sign. Didn't he? What if he didn't? Why did he have to come at me so hard? I apologized. Was that enough? Why wasn't it? He's the one in the wrong. Isn't he? Did I have to use his story? Am I a fraud? Am I a bad person?

I'm not. Am I? What could I have done differently? What could I have said to change his mind? What could I have— No. Stop. This isn't productive.]

But these thoughts swirl through his head.

He tells himself, it's gonna be—

[Okay. It's gonna be okay.]

Finally, he moves. He grabs his phone. Opens Twitter. He doesn't know Eddie's handle, so—he types his own name into the search box. Did Eddie tweet it out like he said he would? Are people talking about him? Is he—

Nothing.

Okay. Okay.

He should feel better. But the thoughts are still there. The questions. The fear.

He gets up. Goes into the kitchen, opens the cupboard, finds a cookie. Eats the cookie.

The cookie doesn't help. The fear's still there. The unknown.

He goes to his bed. Grabs the journal. Stares at the blank page. He doesn't know what to say.

If only—

If only he—

We realize how far gone he is, how much he's lost.

Keith puts down the journal. Looks around his apartment.

He is completely alone.

There's only one thing to do.

He slowly goes to the kitchen.

He retrieves the box of cleaning supplies. Takes out the Pledge, and the rag.

He begins cleaning.

The lights slowly fade.

END OF PLAY

About the Playwright

ERIK PATTERSON is an award-winning playwright, screenwriter, and writing teacher.

His play, *One of the Nice Ones*, earned the Los Angeles Drama Critics Circle Award. His theater work has been produced or developed by Playwrights' Arena, the Los Angeles Theatre Centre, Theatre of NOTE, the Evidence Room, The Actors' Gang, the Echo Theater Company, the Lark Play Development Center, Moving Arts, Black Dahlia, Naked Angels, the Mark Taper Forum, and New Group. His plays have been nominated for the Ovation Award, the Stage Raw Award, the LA Weekly Award, and the GLAAD Media Award.

His writing for TV has been recognized with the Humanitas Prize and the Writer's Guild Award, as well as two Emmy nominations. Along with his writing partner, Jessica Scott, Erik has written films for Warner Bros., Universal, 20th Century Fox, Disney, Freeform, MTV, Paramount, Hallmark, and Syfy, among others. Film and TV credits include: *Abandoned* (starring Emma Roberts and Michael Shannon), *R.L. Stine's The Haunting Hour*, *Another Cinderella Story* (starring Selena Gomez and Jane Lynch), *Deep Blue Sea 2*, *Radio Rebel*, and many more.

Erik is a graduate of Occidental College and the British American Drama Academy. He hosts a gently-guided writing sprint online called "Sunday Sprints" that attracts writers seeking community and inspiration to do their best work.

www.erikpatterson.org

Plays by Erik Patterson

Tonseisha
drama / 1 female, 5 male / 45 minutes, no intermission
A young Japanese woman is haunted by the loss of two men: her father, whom she barely knew, and cult novelist Richard Brautigan, whom she never met. Akiko plays out her father/Richard Brautigan fantasies with a new man nearly every night. Each one of her relationships begins in a bar and ends in a bedroom, and she's never satisfied. She's so lost...can she ever be found?

Yellow Flesh / Alabaster Rose
dark comedy / 5 female, 4 male / full length, one intermission
Elliot is lost in a world of sex workers—late night house calls from hustlers and phone calls with call girls. Becky is torn between two worlds—her day job as a stripper and being a mom to fifteen-year-old Rose (a Goth girl who wants nothing to do with her). And then there's Little B, who has stripped away every piece of herself until all she has left is her obsession with Icelandic pop singer Bjork. This troubled family's shared past holds unspeakable horrors and they must join forces if they ever want to heal. *Winner of the Backstage West Garland Award for Best Playwriting.*

Red Light, Green Light
drama / 6 female, 7 male / full length, one intermission
A gay clown. Two lesbian strippers. A pregnant Goth teen. A deadbeat dad. A horny mother. And a girl who thinks she's Bjork. In this stand-alone sequel to *Yellow Flesh / Alabaster Rose*, the Silverstein family journey towards healing is abruptly halted when Elliot becomes the victim of a brutal gay bashing.

He Asked For It
drama / 1 female, 6 male / full length, one intermission
It's the early 2000s, before PrEP. Ted is new to Los Angeles, and newly out of the closet. He goes on a journey through Hollywood back rooms, nightclub bathrooms, and Internet chat rooms—where he meets and falls in love with Henry. But Henry doesn't yet know how to navigate the dating landscape with his new HIV diagnosis, so he breaks things off with Ted...who then makes a desperate decision to win Henry back. *He Asked For It* asks how far are you willing to go for love? And how much will you forgive? *GLAAD Media Award nominee for Outstanding Los Angeles Theater.*

Sick
dramedy / 3 female, 3 male, 1 child / full length, no intermission
David needs to get laid, Gary could use a drink, and Tim would like you to take your top off. Carla craves cocaine, Jeannie's got God, and Pamela keeps digging herself deeper into the funny and frightening world of hypochondria. But when one of their own gets sick for real, they're all going to have to face their greatest fears and grow up.

I Wanna Hold Your Hand
dramedy / 3 female, 3 male / full length, no intermission
Our lives can change in an instant. One moment you're getting engaged, and a few surreal moments later you're sitting with strangers in an ICU waiting room, praying your fiancé will survive a brain aneurysm. While waiting for Frank to wake from a coma, Ada meets Julia, Paul, and Josh, who are waiting for their mom to wake up. A tenuous friendship is born. *I Wanna Hold Your Hand* looks at life, death, and recovery, and what it means to try your hand at living again...

One of the Nice Ones
dark comedy / 2 female, 2 male / 90 minutes, no intermission
A paraplegic woman plays outrageous power games to get something she desperately wants in this dark, twisty, sexy play that takes office politics to new extremes. *Winner of the Los Angeles Drama Critics Circle Award for Best Playwriting.*

Handjob
dark comedy / 2 female, 4 male / 90 minutes, no intermission
An encounter between a white, gay playwright and his black, straight "shirtless maid" goes disastrously wrong when signals are misinterpreted, lines crossed. *Handjob* explores the aftermath of their meeting, as it reveals deep layers of discrimination, discord, and discontent among people who should be allies. How do you know when you've gone too far if you completely ignore other people's boundaries?

Books by Erik Patterson

Pop Prompts: 200 Writing Prompts Inspired by Popular Music
Available in paperback and e-book

Pop Prompts is a collection of writing prompts that will help you dig deeper and break through creative blocks. Each prompt is paired with a pop song. Let the music be your muse as you work on your memoir, novel, script, poem—or even your own songs. This book can also be a daily jumpstart for therapeutic journaling. Use it however you want, whenever you want. As long as you're writing you're doing it right.

Pop Prompts For Swifties: 99 Writing Prompts
Available in paperback and e-book

Every writing prompt in this book is paired with one of Taylor's songs from the first "era" of her storytelling journey, from her debut album *Taylor Swift* (2006), to *Fearless* (2008), to *Speak Now* (2010), to *Red* (2012), and all the way through *1989* (2014). You don't even have to be a Swiftie—anyone can use these prompts for self-expression and reflection. As a bonus, each prompt includes blank journal pages. Inspiration is only a song away. Put on your favorite Taylor Swift album, pick a prompt, and start writing! Taylor Swift has no involvement in this book. The use of her name is merely descriptive and should not be interpreted as a sign of endorsement.

SUNDAY SPRINTS

Need some motivation?

Do you work better when someone is holding you accountable?

Come to SUNDAY SPRINTS.

Erik Patterson hosts gently-guided writing sprints on Zoom every Wednesday from 6 to 8 p.m. PST and every Sunday from noon to 2 p.m. PST. (Yes, it's called Sunday Sprints on Wednesdays because... why not?)

Here's how it works: I give a new writing prompt every fifteen minutes. You write. That's it.

All sprinters stay on mute. Alone but not alone, you can draw creative energy from the community of writers on your screen. This is a fun, low-pressure environment—a safe space for you to experiment with your writing. No worries: I will never ask you to share your work.

You decide how to use this distraction-free writing time. Work on that screenplay, novel, short story, play, poem, song. Do some therapeutic journaling. Write letters to loved ones. Do some technical writing. Create a D&D campaign. Finish your homework. Seriously, whatever you need to work on.

Let's get that writing done. Together.

Join the Sunday Sprints Patreon at:
www.patreon.com/erikpatterson

Subscribe to the Sunday Sprints mailing list at:
www.erikpatterson.org/sundaysprints

www.ingramcontent.com/pod-product-compliance
Lightning Source LLC
Chambersburg PA
CBHW072059110526
44590CB00018B/3239